New Plains Review

Spring 2016
Editors and Staff

Executive Editor	Shay Rahm
Production Chief	Michelle Lee Waggoner
Editor-in-Chief	Brendon Yuill
Managing Editors	Tami McDaniels
	Anika Johnson
Poetry Editor	Joshua Barnett
Assistant Poetry Editor	Madison Castelli
Fiction Editor	Josh Grizzly Shepard
Assistant Fiction Editors	Ashley Hoffmeier
	Courtney Cullins
	Taylor Cradduck
	Chantell Hay
	Alexis Poindexter
Non-fiction Editor	Megan Biedermann
Assistant Non-fiction Editors	Alexandra Brown
	Widha Gautam
Copy Editors	Ashley Hoffmeier
	Madison Castelli
Social Media Manager	Joshua Barnett
Webmaster	William Andrews

New Plains Review Publishing Group
University of Central Oklahoma
Edmond, Oklahoma

NEW PLAINS REVIEW

ISBN-10: 0-9837357-9-4
ISBN-13: 978-0-9837357-9-3

New Plains Review is a literary journal published each academic semester, sponsored by the English Department, College of Liberal Arts, at the University of Central Oklahoma. The image found on every cover of *New Plains Review* issue since 2000 is based on a painting titled "Phantom Warriors" by acclaimed Native American artist and UCO alumnus Sherman Chaddlesone.

© 2016 by *New Plains Review*

All rights reserved. No part of this publication may be reproduced, distributed, or transmitted in any form or by any means, including photocopying, recording, or other electronic or mechanical methods, without the prior written permission of the publisher, except in the case of brief quotations embodied in critical reviews and certain other noncommercial uses permitted by copyright law. For permission requests, write to the publisher, addressed "Attention: Permissions Coordinator," at the address below.

New Plains Review
English Department, Box 184
University of Central Oklahoma
100 North University Drive
Edmond, Oklahoma 73034
(405) 974-5613

newplainsreview@gmail.com
www.libarts.uco.edu/english/newplains

SUBMISSION INFORMATION: *New Plains Review* accepts original work in poetry, fiction, non-fiction, art, and photography. For submission and editorial guidelines, please visit the website.

ORDERING INFORMATION: Pricing for subscriptions, current and back issues are available through the website.

EQUAL OPPORTUNITY STATEMENT: In compliance with Title VI and Title VII of the Civil Rights Act of 1964, Executive Order 11246 as amended, Title IX of The Education Amendments of 1972, Sections 503 and 504 of The Rehabilitation Act of 1973, the Americans With Disabilities Act of 1990, the Family and Medical Leave Act of 1993, the Civil Rights Act of 1991, and other Federal Laws and Regulations, the University of Central Oklahoma does not discriminate on the basis of race, color, national origin, gender, age, religion, disability, or status as a veteran in any of its policies, practices or procedures; this includes but is not limited to admissions, employment, financial aid, and educational services.

COVER
PHOTOGRAPH
SARAH VOLNER

Foreword

"There *are* no little things. 'Little things,' so called, are the hinges
of the universe."

         – Fanny Fern (Sara Willis)
         Ginger-Snaps

Today, more people than ever before have been able to participate in
the discourse of literature. With the popularization of computers, the
prominence of the internet, and the multitude of platforms available
in the digital medium for artists, writers, and creators, there has been
an almost overwhelming amount of contributions to the literary and
artistic fields in these last few years. The freedom to write, to express,
and to share these works is now more readily available than at any other
moment in history.

This single fact is something that those of us at the *New Plains Review* are
extremely thankful for.

The staff of the *New Plains Review* is comprised of students from the
University of Central Oklahoma — often meeting in a dark conference
room and reviewing the various submissions we receive from all across
the world. And these same submissions impact us in a multitude of ways.
At times, we laugh. At other times, we may frown, or sigh, or perhaps even
launch into a heated debate behind the meaning or merit of the work we
have received. But if there is one constant in the flurry of emotions from
the literature we receive, it is that we always feel grateful.

We feel truly blessed — not only to our contributors for giving us the
privilege to view their works, but to our readership for valuing the works
we select and for giving us their patronage.

With this, we are pleased to present to you the Spring 2016 edition of
the *New Plains Review.*

Brendon Yuill
Editor-in-Chief
New Plains Review

Contents

POETRY

Touching the Transcendent
in Asbury Park

Jeffrey Alfier

Crows follow. Faithful as hell in reproaching me,
though I may be overwrought. In pre-dawn's streetlight
wash and nights of porcelain cups, their off-key clamor
clocks my footsteps. But what the hell do they know,
chewing hoagie crumbs, even half-smoked butts I toss toward
gutters. The penny arcade, disused and vacant,
that's where I hide when Atlantic wind turns my face away
from the sea. I lean against a rifled change machine,
watch a rat breach a corner molding, not six feet away.
Even in this smoke-blue dark it keeps its color of ashen light.
Sirens punctuate my daydreams. Weariness overtakes me.
Right here, next to empties, a torn bra, a bullet casing,
a sign that warns not to loiter. I sit, lean against a corner
below a borax moon that slips the rotting plywood
of a vanished windowpane. Through a half-said
prayer I resume the drift into sleep. I wish the crows
would find the rat, hassle it gone or dead. They won't.

To Ubud

Douglas Cole

far from denial
    far from the snakes of anxiety
        I arrive
under palm trees open
    on a road through villages
        crowded with people
            on bicycles and motorcycles
shopkeepers smoking on stone
    steps leading into shaded huts
        with dust-covered shelves
            loaded with soda cans and water bottles
              packages of dried fruit
and outside a woman drapes her laundry
    across the rocks on the riverbank
        as trash heaps burn on the side of the road
            and smoke sweeps over the fierce face
              demon guarding the temple gate
and banyan trees drape their vines
    over pathways into the Monkey Forest
        as the street narrows down
            to a dirt path and wooden stairs
              where we climb into a courtyard
                lined with Frangipani and Soka
and I think it isn't paradise without you
    but as I follow the path
        around the ponds alive with churling frogs
        and crickets chittering in the darkness
I breathe free of the old injuries
        that kept me clutched in time
        as though I only wore that other
bent under the weight of worry

Such Luck

Sarah Davis

My family has very
active hearts. They
either talk too much or
they're too big.
That's how my dad
went and I've loved
him ever since.

Public Transportation

Alex Hughes

This is not about the glassy-eyed teen across from me,
but the little bit of hope he rolled and smoked, and the money
now sitting in the pocket of someone who doesn't need it,
weighing about the same as a good dinner plate.

This is not about his girlfriend's tongue shoved somewhere
behind the lip of his ear, but the parents who
made her that way — her mother by working two jobs
to keep them afloat, and her father by jumping overboard.

This is not about the suited guy next to me, but the lie
where pinstripes vanish into grime and the truth
he exudes; it's not his shoulder pads, but the way he looks
over them at me from time to time, apologizing.

(This is not about the sheriff nudging a human nest with
the tip of his boot, but an underground bedroom filled
with buzzing lightning bugs, and a mother pushing through
the night, saying, "Honey, it's time for school.")

I don't think it's about the poet handing out poems
titled "Peace," "Hope," and "Love," saying,
"Here, they're free," but the people who
read them, crease them, and throw them away.

It's not about the girl gazing at me from the other end of the car —
not her tattoo sleeve, half-shaved hair, or septum ring, nor
my heart that wishes to be edgier but is too self-aware —
though honestly I wish it could be about that.

(This is not about the race between doors to get
a seat instead of a pole, but the realization that all of life
is a step ahead of death; it's about the millions who place their faith
in the lottery, and the children who yell, "Mine! Mine!")

If I had to guess I'd say it's about the old man sitting quietly —
not the things he sees, but his desire to find
the meaning in them — and how, looking humanity
full in the face, he smiles, determined to be happy.

Junk

Sara Schraufnagel

I asked her how they met over Hamburger Helper
on plastic plates with blue and yellow flowers along
the rim while we drank frosted Cokes she grabbed
from the garage full of boxes, taxidermy equipment and
an old army uniform

Her mom sat silent with vacant eyes,
flicking the last of her ashes out the window
We changed the subject as we both untucked our uniform t-shirts

The last time I saw him he stumbled out of the front door
on a three-day Jack-and-Coke bender
past his two-year-old
as if he was an old dog, a lost interest,
another thing to trip over and leave behind

We sat on the mustard-colored couch that catapulted dust
as soon as you sat down, the same seat I sat in
while her neighbor boy tried to get into my pants with
pervasive hands; he was the one who lived a few blocks down
with four rusted parked cars in the front yard
I knew better to be another forgotten piece of trash
begging to get fixed up or let back inside

I waited to get picked up outside the rusted gate
back to the side of town with fresh cut grass
I saw her circular filter lit up in the darkness
waiting for his truck to pull in any minute

Germination Song

Seth Copeland

As the froth-brimful waves on dunes unfurl,
shaping the beach into hills young with new,
you are the sand grain that gathers the pearl.

The sun leaks a white sky. A boy and girl
walk sideways like crabs. The sand sweats salt dew
as the froth-brimful waves on dunes unfurl.

Consider those specks on which the waves hurl
brine-dank and scurf. So many pasts/futures,
but you are the grain that gathers the pearl.

If lips could spin calligraphy — the curl
of your hair, my mouth, collusion in blue
as the froth-brimful waves on dunes unfurl —

some poem would leak from my shell, a whorl
of nacreous milk, me encoding you
into the sand grain that gathers my pearl.

Foreign stone of this soft mantle, stray burl
mating with my flesh, inveigle me true
as the froth-brimful waves on dunes unfurl,
that you are the grain that gathers the pearl.

If I Could Draw

Lenny DellaRocca

If I could draw
I'd draw shoes

I'd draw the deal
with shoes making
their way to the punch bowl

Shoes for girls with lisps

Shoes pink as balloons
in a five and ten

If I could draw
I'd draw a shoe

A shoe that laughs
like a horse

A slow shoe

A shoe for picking pumpkins

If I could draw
I'd draw shoes

Shoes made of eyelids

Shoes for Algernon

Shoes that look good
in hanky panky soup

If I could draw
I'd draw a shoe

A shoe that gooses   ·
a house

A shoe that whistles
in its sleep

A shoe with pointy
red things

If I could draw
I'd draw shoes

Shoes for dolls
weeping for contentment

Sticky shoes with
pretty tongues

Shoes that play
parlor bingo

If I could draw
I'd draw a shoe

I'd draw a tinsel town shoe

A shoe for war

My last beautiful shoe
that tricked a clown

If I could draw
I'd draw shoes

Shoes for the
Holy Ghost

Shoes to be seen
in Tiffany lamplight

Shoes with the dancing squirts

If I could draw
I'd draw a shoe

A shoe that can
sing "Stardust"

A shoe with a man
in its closet

A shoe with a
nose for news

If I could draw
I'd draw shoes.

Farmer, Clutching Chest

Justin Hamm

The circumstance of his death is nigh.
But as luck would have it, this tragedy
is not without heart; it has gone out ahead
to build an afterlife for him.
Now it stands, silhouetted against a far sunset,
arms raised, waving. The farmer can't see
that far, but he imagines it is smiling.
It wants to know if this is the right place,
this sad plot that seems so much like the harsh
lands he'll soon be leaving.
Yes, he nods, that's the place. He can hardly wait.
He wants to gather all that good soil
in his fingers, to hoard it to himself.
He wants all of it: the inelegance of pig stench
and the garble of good tires treading on gravel road.
Doesn't he understand it will be hard?
He understands. He wants it that way. Is he supposed to
beg for some sort of hoity-toity heaven?
Hell, all he's ever known is hard survival
since the day he set down that fiddle,
and he must know if he can do it there, too —
in the afterlife, where the cruel wind draws itself
from Old Testament sources,
and where the unimaginable drought of eternity
will press constantly against the green edges
of all he dares to grow.
And the woman? Won't he miss the woman?
Mr. Death, you must know very little. She'll be
along this way shortly, will choose the same
as he chose, and for just about the same reasons.
He only hopes he has enough time left
to get everything ready for her. He couldn't stand it
if she got the idea he had been lazing.

A New Communion

Davis Johnson

In the time of Julie Andrews, Pollyanna,
and the Singing Nun, of crisp
high heels on concrete and linoleum,
and hatted men on commuter trains,
a time seemingly prefabbed and
correct as a Swanson TV dinner,
you find yourself 15 and alone
high on a hill in southwest New Hampshire
in a small Catholic boarding school
a Spartan place designed to
make you a worker ant for Christ —
and he works you.

He teaches English and is proctor of the freshman floor,
6'3" of solid oak with an icebreaker intellect:
"Cuba" you say in automatic
recitation of the cold war bromide;
"Russian missile aggression!"
"Turkey," he retorts,
"our bordering missiles, their perception?"
and your geopolitical tectonic plates
make a sudden rumble, and shift.

This is how he works you,
and you feel less alone
unaccountably special even,
despite your glasses, fumblings
and eruptions, and for
the Columbus Day weekend,
he drives you home, out of all
the boys, just you and him;
your parents impressed by how
ever the educator,
he's gone out of his way to bring you to
Harvard's Peabody Museum;
but you don't tell them
of the Greek vases he's led you to,
of Greek youth in heroic poses
sporting heroic hard-ons.
Harvard. High Culture. Hard-Ons.

19

Nor do they hear of the afternoon
after a cross-country run, when
he's joined you in the shower
and asked you to soap up
his thoroughbred back,
and lathering those slabbed layers
of experience, authority,
how rib-caged naked it's made you feel
like a skiff scraping up against a battleship.
This is how the pathogen works its host
In the fresh scrubbed days
of do-re-me and Pollyanna.

It's foggy and cold on the hill
ahead of the blizzards to come
this alien place so far from home
and security; of tormenting classmates
and academic failure;
where the food's so distasteful,
you sometimes drench ketchup between
two pieces of white bread, and eat
pretending a hamburger resides therein.
With the end of the Christmas break,
you've dreaded going back
except he's asked you to return early
to "open up the place,"
just you and him,
and a grateful glow runs through you
reinforced by your parents,
so proud their eldest son's
made such an impression;
isn't this why they've sent you away,
to become a honed, hand-tooled man of God?

The "work" to be done turns out to be little and trivial
until the real project begins to unfold in his small apartment on
the third floor in the deserted
Georgian mansion of a main building
on the hilltop
in the damp and the fog,
where boys are sent to become
Christian Soldiers, to go
out into the world
attached to necktie umbilical cords

to do the good of His One True Church,
Mary Poppins hovering overhead.
But tonight Nannie Patrol is grounded,
as high on the third floor,
IFR conditions prevail:

Thick pleated, leaf brown corduroys.
Button-down shirt.
The casual off-duty uniform
of the prep-school educator.
Classical music in the background, and
"Little Guy," the fat aloof tabby he dotes on.
He pushes a glass on you,
peppermint schnapps;
odd encouragement
In the face of all the warnings
of automatic expulsion
for drinking you've received;
he hands you a girlie magazine
opened up to big-titted ruby lipped bimbos;
so 50s, so not titillating;
Then from the autumn brown corduroys
Emerges the giant he's kept in the barn all evening
kicking at the stalls, now sticking
up like a dead, bark-stripped pitch pine
from a bed of needles;
and it, the schnapps, the bimbos, even Little Guy sprawled in fat
aloofness across the desk,
one eye open
to the proceedings,
await the touch,
the communion.
Awkward, all thumbs
your world a mix of nannies, nuns
Bond, Odd Job,
The biblical Job
and the emerging threat of Pussy Galore;
your meek turn the other cheek
veneer covers hot vole trails of anger
beneath a mind in which the Hardy Boys
sleuth on, surfing surely above
the trough of human suffering of
Dostoyevsky's Crime and Punishment
a book he assigned you;

and you're poised at your own crucible
as he awaits easy and erect,
for an outcome he's prepared for as neatly
as one of his literature lessons.

 You, unprepared, can only find shelter
by playing the idiot,
a role in which you can hide in plain sight,
for you've been pegged there
by your classmates,
even by some of your teachers;
because you've not yet realized
you can create your own world,
as opposed to having it defined by others;
So you cloak yourself in cluelessness,
add a smokescreen of confusion
stammer you're tired, even act a little drunk,
or how you imagine that to be,
and to your great relief,
the pitch pine prong gets stabled
and you're left alone to go to bed.

Only upon awakening to find yourself
more alone than ever.
For as dumb as you played
the night before
your new awareness has
seeped through the subterfuge;
his ripe plum has
taken a crabappleish turn;
You know it.
He knows it.
The attentive tentacles
withdraw, and you're
left in the inky silence
of a bathyscape
cut from its cable and
plunged to the depths of some
Marianas Trench.

Now winter sets in with
northeasterly gales
that drive the fine chaff of snow through
the inadequate defenses of window glaze

to pile in tiny drifts on the inside;
and herd the steam heat to shelter
in hot panic to the leeward side of the building.
Hot and cold you run
as you cling to the world of the Hardy Boys
where no one really gets hurt,
and every crime gets solved,
but no longer can they shelter you
from the existential drafts
of Dostoyevsky, and one January afternoon
full of brittle sun, and wind working
the snow like feeding dolphins
scatter schools of gleaming anchovy;
right after class when you
know he's watching;
you walk out into that foot and a half
of drifted white — jacketless,
the gale whipping your thin tie in your face,
climb onto the garden wall, and stand there —
Waiting.

Sure enough he begged for response:
Full of concern,
a hint of panic even,
he shepherds you back,
at least for the moment
to warmth and shelter.
But at the same time,
more than a call for attention,
you realize something else,
something iron in you
has stepped out on that wall
to test the mettle of cold and wind
and faced it full on
with a shout of refusal
to live life as a scuttling leaf
with no better fate
than to find itself stuck
to some prong on a rake.

A Futile Attempt at Flight

Stefan Strychar

"There is an art to flying . . . learning to throw yourself at the ground and miss."

– Douglas Adams
Life, the Universe and Everything

I threw myself
to miss
Now remiss
I sit with
skinned knee
shaking a fist
at resilient
gravity

Repeat Offender

Rebekah Keaton

Not the first stint in the underbelly
of want. When six, she dabbled:
an older brothers' accomplice at the entrance
of Ames' Department store.
They had recruited her small hands to delve
into the mouths of penny machines, slide
the metal teeth, and drop the forbidden sweet orange
and yellow orbs into their cupped palms.
The three fed windbreakers, Levis, pushed
cheeks out like giant blowfish.

They bartered for ball cards and freezie pops.
In the neighborhood, that summer, there was
a relentless smacking of gum like the ping ping
of throwdown snaps against the sidewalk
where we rode our bikes until the streetlights came on
and we lit out to showers,
possibly prime time.

When she finally got caught, and a mother
stormed down to that dingy office behind
the security plate glass, we heard
she gave them up in an instant,
her brothers.

Part criminal, part narc, for years she played
things close, swearing allegiance to the boy who snuck
his father's car on Saturday nights, or to the stolen kiss
at the end of a dinner party with someone's significant
other. Always the sweet rush of the click clacking lick
against the white picket fence of marriage,
and a mother's dependable recipe
for a potluck casserole.

In her defense, I hoarded her love notes, too,
Like gumdrops, fully culpable, always,
to the sugar rush.

VISUAL ART

Depression

Morgan Bradley

Jewelry

Nina Nga Nguyen

Rocks

Nina Nga Nguyen

Koi Fish

Nina Nga Nguyen

Untitled

Sarah Volner

Untitled

Sarah Volner

FICTION

Wish You Were Here

Riley Bounds

It was nightfall by the time Huey crossed into Franklin County. Evergreens and the skeletons of birches blocked the sky. He seemed lost along a path that wound and coiled upon itself like Penrose steps leading into a world of blackness. The headlights of the aged Nissan coupe flickered on occasion and spared little luminescence to guide him there. He was swallowed in a foreign land.

He oftentimes looked at her in the urn strapped in the passenger's seat by the seat belt. He would reach from the gearshift to caress its lid and marble siding. He would look at it with his mouth somewhat ajar and stare for some time before returning his attention to the road. He reached for her again and touched the urn.

The impact swayed the trees along the roadsides. The SUV pushed the coupe through the intersection and on up the embankment of a drainage ditch. Huey had to look at the clump of cloth and sponge in his hand before it registered that he'd torn a piece of the fabric lining out of the ceiling. He looked and saw the passenger's side door bent in, concave towards him. The urn had tipped to its side but retained its lid. He looked in his rearview mirror at the SUV stopped behind his car. Its headlights were gone and the whole of its front end was crushed in. Its radiator steamed. A man and his wife exited the vehicle, and in the dimness of his brake lights they seemed disoriented but unharmed.

Huey looked about him a moment and discovered the center console again. He opened it and produced his insurance card. He looked at the expiration date. His coverage had expired a month ago. Huey regarded this and looked wide-eyed behind his thick spectacles into the rearview mirror again. The wife cried out of shock and the husband held her steady. He watched them and daintily shifted into reverse. He backed out of the gully and onto the pavement. "Hey," the man from the SUV called. Huey slipped into drive. Through his shattered passenger window he heard the man hollering and swearing after him as he scooted along the road, the passenger's side front wheel grating, not headed in any particular direction in that algid night.

The woman with the glandular problem and pink plastic-rimmed glasses and a mountain of hair held together by intricate passes with a can of hairspray read her *People* magazine behind the reception desk. The heater choked and sputtered through vents with fans too rusted to oscillate. Bon Jovi drowned most of it in "Livin' on a Prayer." When Huey pulled into the parking lot, she heard the wailing of the warped metal against the ball bearing and bent her magazine in half to look out the glass front doors laden in condensate. The cacophony diminished into a hissing and ended as Huey shut the engine off. She looked out a while before she straightened her magazine and blew a bubble of her gum.

Huey walked into the main office. She didn't look up as he approached the desk.

"Could I get a room for the night?" Huey asked.

She brought forth a laminated sheet stained with permanent marker and streaks of erasing. "Just one night?"

"Yes."

She traced a pink polymer resin nail across the sheet. "Well you're in luck. There's one room left." She set the sheet aside and passed him a clipboard. He filled in his information. When he was done he handed it back to her. She reviewed it. "Dr. Herbert Huey," she read. She lowered the clipboard to look at him. "You got a practice around here?"

"I'm not that kind of doctor."

She chewed her gum and looked at him. "What kinda doctor are ya then?"

"Ph.D. Philosophy."

Her lower mandible moved to and fro as a cow chewing its cud. "So you're not a real doctor then, huh?"

He looked at her. She inflated a pink bubble and it burst. She collected it into her orifice again. "What room did you say that was?" Huey asked.

She leaned back and the chair moaned under her weight. She retrieved a set of keys and passed them to him. "Room one fifty-five," she said. "We'll charge your card."

"Thank you." He turned to leave. On his way to the door, he noticed an espresso machine plugged in atop a splintered wooden table laden with magazines and maps. "You all have coffee?" he asked.

"That's what the machine's for," she said behind her magazine.

He studied the machine. He pressed a button and a blue LED screen illuminated. He tepidly pressed another button and the screen cycled through a myriad of options – espresso shot, frappe, mocha, hot chocolate, etc.

He looked back at her. "Is there just a coffee option on this thing?"

She bent her magazine backwards and glared at him. "It's all coffee. It's a coffee machine."

"I know, but what about just plain coffee?"

She looked at him. Her glasses slipped down to her rounded nose. "It's *all coffee*."

He looked at her and then at the machine and sighed.

◞

Huey gathered her urn from the car and carried her under the sparse light of incandescent bulbs to Room 155. He turned the key in the lock and had to jostle the handle before it opened. He came in and turned the lights on, and the girl under the sheets of the queen-size mattress sat erect with her pistol drawn and trained on him. Huey's eyes enlarged.

"Who are you?" she said.

"Dr. Herbert Huey," he said slowly. He clenched the urn.

"What've you got in your hands?"

He looked down at the urn and back at the girl. "My daughter," he said.

The girl furrowed her brow a moment before motioning with her head and the pistol and saying, "Put her on the dresser."

Huey looked at the chest of drawers beside the entrance and gently placed the urn atop it.

"Now raise your hands," she said. He did so, shaking. "How'd you get in?" she said.

"With a key."

"What kinda key?"

"Apparently the kind you get from inattentive office workers."

"What?"

"I got it from the office. The lady said this was the only free room."

She shook her head and sighed and flung the covers off herself and moved with the pistol still aimed at him towards the closet. She slipped a heavy jacket over her pajamas. She walked to the door and said, "Move."

Huey stood with his hands above him. "I would," he said at length, "but I don't think I can move my legs."

She scoffed and shouldered past him. She holstered the pistol in one of the jacket pockets.

"Why'd you give us the same room?" the girl said.

"Must've forgotten to mark yours off," the receptionist said behind her *Vogue* magazine.

"So there's no rooms available?" Huey said.

"Seems that way," the receptionist said and turned the page.

"Well, are you gonna refund us or not?"

"You could always share."

Huey and the girl looked at each other. Then the girl leaned forward on the reception counter. "I'm not sharing a room with some old geezer I just met."

Huey made a face. "I'm fifty-two," he muttered.

The receptionist inhaled sharply and looked up at Huey. "We'll reimburse your charge in the morning."

The girl turned and left. Huey watched her before turning back to the counter. "So where am I supposed to stay then?"

Huey cradled himself in the driver's seat of the Nissan, his legs drawn up to his chest and arms wrapped about them. He shivered in his sleep and the clouds of his shuddering breaths trailed up and beyond him and dissipated as quickly as they'd been emitted. He dreamt of her that night, the girl in the urn in the passenger's seat. She stood atop the dormitory tower overlooking the campus and the city beyond, miniature Babels in man's attempt to reach God or at least find what they believe in. The sun resurrected against the skyscrapers and glass palaces and archaic clock towers to touch her silken hair fluttering into the current of a winter wind, and the sun warmed them both. She turned again to face him and smiled.

The girl rapped on the driver's side window and jolted him awake. He looked up at her through the glass. She held a guitar case. He checked the urn in the passenger's seat. He squinted in the early morning light and engaged the car battery and rolled the window down.

"Yes?"

"You stay out here all night?"

Huey sighed and rubbed against his eyes. "Mmhm."

"Where're you headed?"

"Syracuse." He blinked a few times before he said, "I don't even know what town I'm in."

"Waverly."

"Oh."

"Seems like you had a bad night."

He looked at her, chin pressed into his jacket and eyes narrowed as his breath clouded and faded above the half of the vehicle he had left. "You don't say," he said.

"I wanna come with you."

"What?"

"I wanna go with you to Syracuse."

"Why?"

"It's full of people I don't know."

He stared at her a moment before he said, "That makes no sense."

"I sing," she said and gestured with the guitar case. "I need new gigs. I have to put my name out there somehow."

He stared at her. "You threatened to shoot me — " He checked the digital clock on the radio. " — six hours ago."

"You came into the room I was staying in six hours ago."

"How old're you anyway?"

"Old enough." She bumped the roof of the car with her palm. "Open up so I can get in."

"Go around the other side."

She looked around the windshield to the passenger's side, the warped metal and the door bent in like an empty pore and the hull of the car almost torn off. "You're joking, right?"

He noted this as well and nodded. "Right." He exited the driver's side and reclined the seat forward to admit access to the backseat. She set her guitar case along the floorboard and climbed in. He boarded again and started the car. "Do I at least get your name?" he asked.

"Emily."

"Emily," he repeated. He shifted into reverse. "That's pretty. I don't know many Emilys nowadays."

"It's over a hundred miles to Syracuse. You think this'll hold up that long?"

"I suppose we'll find out."

"You said you're a doctor, right?"

"Not the kind you're thinking. I have a Ph.D. in Philosophy." He backed out and faced the exit of the parking lot and shifted into drive.

"Then you're not a real doctor. I mean, you know that, right?"

They rolled forward ten feet before the passenger's side front wheel snapped off at the axle and the car ground its front bumper against the concrete to a halt. The wheel rolled a ways and hit a curb and toppled. "So I've heard," he sighed.

The wrecker came after Huey called from the main office. They towed the Nissan to their yard the next town over. They charged over a hundred dollars a day for its security and maintenance. Huey told them to keep it and paid a one-time fee.

Huey and Emily waited outside for their taxi, their total luggage an urn and a guitar case. They sat without speaking under a cold opaque expanse, lineaments of clouds overhead with no definite form.

"You think it'll snow?" Emily asked at one point, looking overhead.

"Eventually."

The taxi arrived within a half hour. Emily loaded her guitar in along the backseat floorboard, and as Huey lowered into the car to secure the urn, Emily drew her pistol. Huey looked from the barrel to her.

"Sorry doc, but this is as far as we're going together," she said.

Huey looked over at the taxi driver and knocked on the front passenger's window. "Hey, you seeing this?"

"Nope," the driver called.

Huey sighed and faced her.

"Wallet," Emily said and tipped the pistol at him. "Now."

Huey produced the wallet from his back pocket and held it out. She took it. She reached inside the cab and set the urn at his feet. She loaded into the cab and rolled the window down before they drove out of the lot. "Hope you get her to Syracuse," she said.

The taxi drove away south. Huey watched her depart and picked up the urn. He brushed the particles of gravel from the bottom and looked back at the main office. Then he turned south again and walked out alongside the road.

By midafternoon he reached Lake Clear following Highway 30 and a set of train tracks nearby. On the edge of the lake he seated himself and set the urn beside him on the jaundiced grass and watched the black undulations of the water's surface circumambulate and reach for his feet, trying to draw him in. He sat here in the stillness of this place and placed a hand on the urn.

From the north he heard the bellowing of a horn.

Huey ran alongside the freight train with the urn held about his middle, waddling along as a duck startled. He cast glances over his shoulder for the next open shipping container. One appeared from behind him; "Black Spades" was graffitied along its length. Huey propelled himself up, urn first, onto its ledge. He caught one of the walls before he could fall out and flailed his legs out behind him until he wormed his way inside the storage unit. He checked the urn; it was intact.

He got to his feet and looked about the unit. The shadows held nothing until he heard a click and looked to the front of the holding. A man with hair slick as wet tar and a tatterdemalion Superman T-shirt beneath a brown jacket pocked in cigarette burns and torn cargo pants aimed a revolver at him.

Huey sighed. "What is it with you people?"

The man chuckled. "Don't worry bout it," he said and pulled the trigger. The hammer clicked. "Haven't had any bullets for it in a year or so now," the man told him.

"Why keep it then?"

"Why keep a dead person in a jar?"

Huey said nothing.

"Sit," the man said.

Huey acquiesced.

"Where ya headed, stranger?" the man said.

"Syracuse."

"What's in Syracuse?"

"Syracuse University."

"And what's there for you at a university?"

"Nothing."

"Then why go?"

Huey nudged the urn in his lap. "For her."

The man nodded.

"What's your name?" Huey asked.

44

"Jeremiah. Least it used to be."

"Have you been on the rails a long time?"

"I dunno. Twenty years, maybe. You lose track of the winters."

"Why do you ride?"

"Why do you?"

"I don't."

"Then why're you here?"

Huey looked at him. "I got mugged."

"Mm."

"Why don't you go home?"

"Had one." Jeremiah looked out at the black depths of the lake and the ashen cavity of the heavens above. "It was taken from me." He sighed and smiled somber. "Guess I'm like Diogenes. Everywhere's my home now. Wherever I wind up."

Huey looked at him. "You know Diogenes?"

"'The Dog'? Yeah. Studied him a while at university when I was young." Jeremiah chuckled. "Never knew I'd get to know the subject of my master's thesis so well."

Huey shook his head. "What're you doing on this train, man?"

Jeremiah smiled. "Seeing the world."

They rode together into the last refracting lights of sun off the waters of Lake Oneida.

"Nietzsche was full of himself," Jeremiah said. He bit into his half of a moon pie he'd saved and split with Huey. He picked away bits of it from his beard. "You could pretty easily make a case for him being an Ubermensch by his own theories."

Huey laughed and motioned at him. "You don't buy into the Ubermensch? You're wearing his shirt."

Jeremiah looked down at his Superman shirt. "I wear his shirt so I don't freeze to death."

Huey chuckled and looked out the container at the lake as they passed along. "How long does this train go anyway?"

"Till Rushville, last I heard."

Huey looked at him. "Rushville? That's almost fifty miles west of Syracuse."

"That's Lake Oneida. Syracuse is right on the other side of it."

Huey stood and looked out the door. The train now crossed onto a bridge suspended over the water.

"Hold the lid fast when you jump and keep your feet pointed down."

Huey looked back at Jeremiah. He stood before him holding the urn out to him. Huey took it and nodded. He walked to the ledge of the opening and steadied himself. The water was thirty feet down and black, crawling. There was less than two hundred feet of bridge left before the

45

oncoming precipice. Huey leapt forth and dove feet first into the water, clasping the urn to his chest like a life preserver. The water beat and enveloped him, and it stung his skin, the bitter cold of it. He resurfaced and in the waning dusk he saw Jeremiah standing in the container opening watching for him before it disappeared beyond the edge of the cliff.

Huey stripped himself of the jacket, carrying the bulk of the water weight his clothes had absorbed. He shivered in this cold upon the cold of the impending night. He rounded the embankment of the lake to the south side, rubbing his arms and chest. He crested the ridge and looked out over the farmland, lulling itself in winter's requiem. The pink striations of sunlight bled back into themselves over the rampart of the world's horizon as darkness became the firmament. In these last lights, Huey looked and beheld a white donkey drinking at the water's edge.

"Come on," Huey pleaded. The donkey meandered along the side of the lake, ears flattened. Huey followed alongside it and tried more than once to fling his leg over the animal's back. When he'd almost mount, the donkey would cry and rear up and he would slide off. Finally he held the urn and watched the donkey totter up the ridge and over the hillock. As it descended the other side, Huey flung himself from the apex of the mound and landed atop the donkey's back, urn cradled between his armpit and side, and arms lashed about the creature's neck. The donkey brayed and ran variegated to and fro for some time, bucking and kicking at Huey. In time it exhausted itself and wandered ahead towards the lights of the city.

It was five miles from the vale into Syracuse. When they reached the first stretches of concrete, Huey dismounted the burro and slapped it on its rear. It kicked at him and snorted and trod off.

Huey wandered the streets teeming with neon amid shops in nooks and crannies of brick and cinder block buildings and crowds of people moving along in waves against each other. There were such lights that they hardly betrayed shadows. Huey passed an alleyway and caught a glimpse of a stained and threadbare orange Syracuse University blanket dangling from a dumpster. He shook it out and draped it over his shoulders. His clothes were still damp.

It was past midnight before Huey found the spires of the Crouse College peeking out over a hill hidden by the surrounding buildings. He smiled and caressed the side of the urn with his thumb.

꩜

On his way to the university campus he stopped while passing a cathedral. He looked at the stained glass atop the foremost spire and couldn't remember how long it'd been since he'd entered a church. He ascended the leaden concrete steps and passed through the heavy wooden doors.

Huey walked the aisle through the sanctuary past the pews and the scattered few who knelt in prayer behind them. He made his way into the confessional and seated himself in the dim confines of the box. The priest sat beyond the lattice, some solemn divinity behind a veil.

"Bless me, Father, for I have sinned."

"What are your sins, my son?"

"Well, I'll admit, it's been so long since I've been to a church I can't remember when I last spoke to God. I think somewhere along the way I gave up on the idea."

"The idea of what?"

"Higher power."

"You don't see the order of the world? The intricacy of things?"

Huey chuckled. "Order in the disorder?"

"We see but as through a veil."

Huey stared at his knees. "The second law of thermodynamics states that everything is headed from a state of order to disorder. You see that, Father?"

"He will never leave us or forsake us."

"You sure about that?"

"That's the object of faith."

"Huh. Oh yeah, I bet on the Giants a few times. If it's any penance, I lost."

The priest seemed puzzled.

"I actually came in here more to ask you a question than anything else."

"Speak, my son."

"When you get a parent coming in here asking you about where God was after their kid shot themselves, and they can't sleep because the dreams are worse than when they're awake, and they blame themselves and God and anyone else they can pull into it, what do you tell them?"

The priest was silent a moment before he said, "I would tell them He lost a Son once too."

The priest provided Huey with a set of dry baptism robes. He rid himself of his outfit and blanket. Walking the streets in near translucent robes, he felt a little embarrassed, but they were warm enough and dry. At about three in the morning as he neared the college campus, he saw a blackboard out front of a coffee shop that read in different shades of chalk: "LOCAL TALENT TONIGHT: COMPLIMENTARY COFFEE."

"We have mocha soy bean latte, vanilla latte, vanilla frappe, the pumpkin spice latte is our biggest seller, espresso…"

Huey stood in his resplendent robes and shook his head at the barista. "I just want a coffee," he said pitifully.

The tapping at the microphone bumped through the speakers and drew his attention. On the stage at the back of the shop, Emily was getting situated while the crowds paid her no mind. She seated herself atop the stool in front of the microphone stand and lowered the set to her level. She cradled the guitar in her lap. "Um, hi everyone," she said in a quiet voice that Huey could barely make out over the hum of the crowd. "My name's Emily King, and, um, this is 'Hallelujah' by Leonard Cohen." And she played the first eight measures before singing in a dulcet alto:

"Well, I heard there was a secret chord
David played and it pleased the Lord,
But you don't really care for music, do ya?
Well, it goes like this: the fourth, the fifth,
The minor fall, the major lift,
The baffled king composing Hallelujah…
Hallelujah, hallelujah
Hallelujah, hallelujah."

And in this way she sang, and the crowd simmered to whispers and low voices as they watched her. Huey looked on, and despite himself, he smiled.

Emily finished the last refrain and said, "Thank you," into the microphone before heading down front of the stage. The audience cheered and clapped for her, and she blushed. She paled when she saw Huey there in a white sheet like a child's nightmare.

"I want my wallet back," Huey said to her across their table.
"And why would I give it back?"
"I think there's more to you than thievery."
"How would you know that?"
"I just heard you."

She bit at her lip and exhaled and drew the wallet out of her back pocket. She slid it to him. "I'm sorry. I just do what I have to do."
"And what is it you have to do?"
"Make my way. Somehow."
"What're you trying to prove, Emily? Who're you trying to show up with all your toughness?"

She was looking off at the front of the shop, at some potted fern against the window. "One of my first interviews with agents," she said, "the guy asked me, 'You know how pop singers make it?' And he ... but I wouldn't. I wouldn't." She wiped her nose on her sleeve. "I'll find my way by myself. I always have."

Huey looked at her a while. She looked out at the street, at the masses walking by, talking with each other, laughing. "I want you to come with me to the university," Huey said. He smiled at her.

She narrowed her brow at him. "Why?"

He only smiled. "Bring your guitar, all right?"

Huey pushed through the heavy iron door and stepped out atop the Brewster Hall Tower. He led Emily through with her guitar. He held the urn.

They walked near the edge of the building overlooking the rolling dales of the campus, the city and its waning artificial suns as dawn broke over the horizon. Huey's white baptism robes fluttered in the winter breeze. "She was enrolled here for this semester," he said, looking out where the valley ended at the beginning of the concrete world. "She was supposed to move in here, in this tower." He looked down at his daughter in the urn. He cried but kept his composure enough to ask, "You know 'Wish You Were Here,' by Pink Floyd?"

"Of course."

He looked back at her, shaking. "It was her favorite."

Emily removed the guitar from its case and laid the case aside and strapped it about her shoulder. As the sun rose and Huey faced the dawn she played the measures and sang:

> *"So, so you think you can tell*
> *Heaven from Hell?*
> *Blue skies from pain?*
> *Can you tell a green field*
> *From a cold steel rail?*
> *A smile from a veil?*
> *Do you think you can tell?"*

And Huey cried for her. He pressed the urn against his forehead and wept for what was and never was.

> *"How I wish, how I wish you were here.*
> *We're just two lost souls swimming in a fish bowl*
> *Year after year.*
> *Running over the same old ground.*
> *What have we found?*
> *The same old fears.*
> *Wish you were here."*

He sobbed and whispered, "Oh, baby. Why didn't you just talk to me?"

Emily watched him there on the building's edge against the breaking dawn and strummed the last chords for him. Huey found the strength to loosen the lid and held it at his side, gazing into the orifice of the urn and the shadows within. As Emily played he gently waved the urn over the arc of the horizon, and the wind carried her ashes into the sun.

The Fortune Teller

April Vázquez

On the day they were to see the fortune teller, José made arrangements to get off work early. There was always more work in Don Trino's shop than there were hours to do it, and most evenings José didn't get home until after nine o'clock. By the time he'd eaten and showered, the fortune teller would have long since closed up.

Don Trino had listened to his petition with an amused smile. "A fortune teller, you say?"

"I don't believe in it," José insisted defensively. "It's just that Marisol wants me to take her."

Don Trino shook his head and walked away, still smiling into his moustache, but he let José have the afternoon off. José was his best worker and had been with him since he was fourteen years old. For years, until he finished *la preparatoria,* the young man went to school in the mornings and worked at the shop afternoons and weekends. Most of the *muchachos* had little education — a couple hadn't even finished primary school — but José had graduated with high marks and could have gone to the university if he hadn't crossed the Rio Grande instead, looking for an opportunity to make fast money.

He'd spent twenty-seven months in *el norte* before rejoining Don Trino full-time at the shop. During that time, José had saved up enough money to buy a car — used, slightly dented, with one window that wouldn't open, but a car in any case — and to convert the back patio of his father's house into a suite of two rooms for himself and his bride. He spent the last of his *dólares* on their wedding. It was a point of pride with the young man that he'd been able to hire *mariachis* to play at the reception. No one among all of Marisol's married sisters and cousins had ever had *mariachis.*

All of her sisters were married except Magdalena, the youngest. José usually found the girl at his father's house when he arrived in the evenings, flat on her stomach watching television with Marisol, a bag of *churritos* in her hand. It always irritated him to see her sprawling there with such familiarity, talking with her mouth full, on their bed. The truth was that José was jealous of Magdalena. She and Marisol were *como uña y mugre,* as the saying went — *like fingernail and filth* — and José knew which of them was the filth. He resented having to walk Magdalena to the bus stop, three full blocks away, almost nightly. He already had so little time with Marisol! It seemed to him that Magdalena deliberately dawdled, the hint of a smirk on her face, as she stuffed her books into her backpack and kissed her sister goodbye. But he felt it would be churlish of him to mention his feelings, especially since Marisol was left with the responsibility of caring for José's blind father while he worked. He knew she enjoyed her sister's visits, the two of them giggling like little girls over gossip or engrossed in their *telenovelas*. José loved his wife's tinkling laugh, the rows of straight white teeth visible, and her great, sparkling black eyes. The last thing he wanted was to make her unhappy.

That was why he was willing to take her to the fortune teller. The idea was a bit ridiculous to him, embarrassing even, and his mother — *may she rest in peace* — would certainly have disapproved, but Marisol seemed so eager to go that he couldn't bring himself to refuse her. Also José thought he'd noticed a kind of listlessness in her manner lately, an absent-mindedness that he wasn't accustomed to, and that made him uneasy. Twice he'd come home to find the beans, caked and black, burned in the bottom of the *olla*, and Marisol seemed to have completely given up refilling little Torito's food and water bowls on the floor of his father's bedroom. With her husband, she was as faithful to her duties as ever, as much in the bedroom as in the rest of the house, but he felt that some subtle change had taken place. Maybe the fortune teller could help her sort out whatever it was.

José wondered if she might be pregnant. It seemed to him that there had been little clues over the past few weeks. The night he found her standing in front of the full-length mirror in the bedroom looking sideways at her body. An *antojo*, just the other night, for guava ice cream that could only be satisfied by his going out in the rain, at bedtime, to the *nevería*. And there was another possible clue as well. Marisol had stopped taking communion at Mass these last few weeks. José speculated that she worried there was something sinful in hiding the news from him, almost like lying. When he'd suggested that they go to church early the previous Sunday to make their confessions, she hadn't wanted to: he was sure it was because she didn't want to confess until after she'd told him about the baby.

It was so like her not to tell him the news right away, to savor the knowledge, to want the surprise to have the greatest possible impact. The idea endeared her all the more to José. *I'll let her have her secret,* he told himself languidly, imagining her squeals of delight when she finally did tell him. *I'll make a big show of it when I hear the news, give her the pleasure of thinking she surprised me. I won't let on that I knew all along.*

The fortune teller lived at 415 Avenida Endor, in the *colonia* Santa Rita. José took the wrinkled scrap of paper with the address from his pocket and smoothed it out across the middle of the steering wheel. He knew the area, having made occasional calls for work to a factory on Avenida la Revolución a few streets away. The rain beating on the windshield of the car dappled the paper, making it look as though Tía Claudia's neat blue letters were under attack by a band of shadowy liquid assailants. It was the seventeenth consecutive day of rain. This was how León was: for three-quarters of the year the weather was absolutely Edenic, then the whole summer long it rained heavily every day — hard, steady rains that began in the afternoon and continued throughout the night, soaking the ground and causing flash floods — as if all the accumulated wrath of the heavens were being unleashed at once.

For José the drive was marked by a sense of excitement. Not because of the fortune teller — they might have been going anywhere — but because it was so rare for the two of them to be out alone, doing something together that they'd never done before. What did it matter if the man was a charlatan, as he must surely be? José was taking Marisol to him. His chest felt suffused with the warmth of pride and satisfaction: she wanted it, and he was able to make it happen.

Reaching over for his wife's hand, he began earnestly, "*Amor*, you know you shouldn't put too much stock in what this fellow tells you, eh?"

"What makes you say that, *corazón*? Tía Claudia swears by him."

"Well, it's just that telling people terrible things is their bread and butter, these fortune tellers."

"But he told Auntie a very good thing. He told her that she was going to be a grandmother, even before Aracely knew she was pregnant with Hernán."

José turned away and smiled knowingly to himself. To his wife he said, "Well, that's just it, isn't it? That's a pretty general prediction for a woman of Tía Claudia's age."

"But he knew the baby would be a boy!"

Was that what this was about, then? Sweet Marisol, worried that José would be disappointed with a girl child. A surge of tenderness shot through him, and he reminded himself to stress to her, when the time came, how happy he'd be with a child of either sex.

"If he were to predict some catastrophe, I just don't want you to panic, my love. You must go into it with the idea that you won't believe a word he says."

They pulled up to the curb outside the façade of an unremarkable brown block house. José let himself out of the car, straddling a puddle, then huddled his wife onto the sidewalk under the awning. Almost as soon as he'd rung the bell, the door opened to reveal a large woman with wide hips and a round, impassive face. A collection of small, dark moles scattered across her cheeks gave her the look of having been spattered with mud.

"His seven o'clock?" the woman asked brusquely, giving José and Marisol a cursory looking-over.

They both nodded. With a gesture, she indicated the doormat, where the two young people carefully wiped their wet feet, then she turned and lead them through the front room of the house. It smelled faintly of something fried, traces of the midday meal lingering weakly in the stale air, and José looked around him with interest, noting that the room didn't give any indication of mysticism on the part of its owner. There was an old television set in one corner, an arrangement of dusty silk flowers on a coffee table, a curio cabinet filled with ornate perfume bottles on yellowed doilies. He wondered vaguely what he'd expected.

Upon reaching the doorway to the next room, the woman, whom José had mistaken for the help, called out tonelessly, "Your seven o'clock, *querido*," then, showing them in with an extended hand, she turned on her heel and closed the door behind her.

This room was smaller and darker than the long, brightly lit front room of the house. There was a close smell, such as might emanate from the body of an animal, and the air felt dense, as though someone had recently showered there. Dozens of candles in different-colored glass cylinders threw their light, patchwork, over the scene. The fortune teller, who'd been seated at a small, cluttered table, rose and offered each of them his hand. He was a big man, balding, with a fringe of graying hair like a privet hedge around the shiny surface of his head and the same thickset features as his wife. He looked like a transit officer, or a butcher, and José again asked himself what he'd expected. This time he had an answer: he'd imagined someone lithe and willowy, with flowing locks and a long beard. Someone otherworldly. He stole a glance around the room, which was filled with books, statues and images of Catholic saints, and dozens of glass canisters of dried herbs.

"The charge for the consultation will be *doscientos pesos*," the fortune teller announced frankly, eyeing José expectantly over the rims of his bifocal lenses. The young man pulled out his wallet and passed the bill across the table. "Have a seat."

They both moved forward and sat down in the metal folding chairs before them, but at once Marisol turned anxiously to her husband. Her eyes wide in the candlelight, she asked him in a low voice, "You're going to wait outside, aren't you?"

"What?" José stared at her.

"I just thought — " Marisol began, but the fortune teller had already begun speaking. She broke off and looked nervously in his direction.

"The two of you are newly married, just beginning your life together, yes?"

"Yes," José answered quickly, not looking at his wife.

"And you're thinking of starting a family."

"Yes," José said again.

"The time is not propitious. I recommend against it." He inclined his head toward José. "You have an aged relative, someone who depends on you, I believe?"

"It's my father," José said, surprised. "He's blind. My sister was caring for him, but she moved to Aguascalientes after she married."

"And you've lost your mother, haven't you?"

"Yes," José answered with audible astonishment. "She — she died while I was away from home."

"She's at peace," the fortune teller said succinctly. "It's important to her that you know that."

José felt his throat tighten. It was the greatest regret of his life that he had not been at his mother's side during her last days.

"But — " the fortune teller said abruptly in a different tone, pulling a card from the Tarot deck before him with a quick motion, almost that of a magician. "*You're* here tonight for a different reason."

He peered at Marisol over his glasses and declared peremptorily, "You've come because you're anxious about something you've done." A pause. "Something you aren't proud of."

The fortune teller made eye contact with José before going on in a lower voice.

"Betrayal."

He laid the card face-up on the table before them. It featured two figures: the disgraced Adam and Eve, their naked bodies as smooth and hairless as a pair of Xoloitzcuintli dogs. In the air between them, a fiery-haired angel rose out of a billowing mass of cumulonimbus clouds, its purple wings tinged with blazing scarlet. Eve's anguished eyes were turned supplicatingly on the angel above her; Adam's were fixed on her. Two words in thick black letters, punctuated with a period, ran the length of the card below them like an indictment: THE LOVERS.

José's body went completely cold, then, almost as quickly, hot. Around him the candlelight flickered like a convocation of spirits, and his heart beat wildly as though in communion with the rain that pounded on the roof with renewed fury. The fortune teller went on, something about forgiveness and reconciliation, but José hardly heard. It was as if all the air had been sucked from the room, as if a light had gone out, as if somewhere, far away, a star had imploded upon itself and forever altered the balance of the entire universe. His Marisol! He glanced sideways at his wife's candlelit face, but her placid features gave no sign of anything amiss. José thought he might be sick.

He looked around him for something on which to concentrate, the way spinning *bailarinas* focus on a fixed point to maintain their equilibrium. Looking to his right, his eyes met the gaping eyeholes in the skeletal face of *La Santa Muerte,* draped, in this version, in the starry vestment of Our Lady of Guadalupe. The skull leered at him, its folded hands clasped to its breast in a mockery of prayer. The two upward points of the crescent moon at its feet were like animal horns, José realized in horror: like the horns Marisol had put on him. He quickly looked away from the image, catching sight instead of the steady brown eyes of Saint Dymphna in white robes across him on the far wall. She looked upon him fixedly, appealingly, but José lowered his head and closed his eyes against her.

After some final words of advice for Marisol on how to strengthen her aura, the fortune teller stood. Taking one of the glass canisters from the shelf behind him, he began to fill a small plastic bag with dried herbs, intoning, as he did so, a series of instructions for the making of a tea. Then, with another moist handshake for both of them, the fortune teller summoned his wife — "Eufemia! Can you show these *jovenes* out?" — and they were dispatched.

The couple followed the woman's voluminous buttocks back the way they'd come, blinking in the sudden bright light of the front room. Before she opened the front door, Eufemia paused and stood for a moment looking at José, an ironic smile playing about her lips. As she reached for the door handle, she asked mildly, "I imagine you'll be back?" It wasn't quite a question.

He nodded numbly and stumbled back out onto the wet sidewalk. The rain, which had been falling in torrents only moments before, had now stopped completely, and the only sound was the dripping of rainwater from the *tejas* of the housetops. A ghostly mist rose up from the hot pavement as if the souls of the dead, invoked by séance, were gathering for a convergence upon the living.

Fumbling with the keys, José opened the car door for his wife, then walked around and lowered himself limply into the driver's seat. At once Marisol cried gaily, "Well, *amor*, you couldn't have been more right about that fellow! He didn't know anything at all!" Her tinkling laugh rang out in the silence, but for José the sound was hollow. Marisol was lost to him now, ruined, Eve after Eden.

He gripped the steering wheel with both hands, staring through the rain-spattered windshield in front of him. The key remained unturned in the ignition. The sudden cessation of rain after so many hours gave the empty street before them an almost preternatural calm. But it was an expectant stillness: a stillness pregnant with the promise of a storm to come.

Roosevelt

W. Scott Thomason

I'm going down to the creek to catch Jubal a turtle.

Everyone's talking about him and the strike at the mill and what a fine thing he did so he needs something special. Daddy says Jubal's not gotten what he's owed. I think I owe him a turtle.

I get dizzy because I'm weak in the blood, but Jubal helped me and said I can do anything. He taught me how to catch turtles down at the creek. He showed me where to dig a hole and where to put the lettuce from the icebox. Jubal said that when the turtle fell in that I could hold him for a little while but that a turtle's like a man, and just because you pick him up doesn't mean he's yours to keep. A turtle feels cool like the water. When I'm weak in the blood a turtle feels good. Jubal said that I can catch turtles even if the world is spinning.

A turtle is a special present and Jubal is special because he's my brother and he stood with the strikers against Mr. Tillman and his men.

Last time we were at the creek Jubal gave me a ribbon like the one he was wearing. He said I can't wear it when the men from the mill are around but I can keep it in my pocket. There's a meeting at the church with the men from the mill and Daddy's gone there and he's been yelling about Mr. Roosevelt and the government. Mama says I have to stay inside, but I know how to use the window. Mr. Roosevelt's the president and that makes Daddy yell. So I'm going down to the creek to catch Jubal a turtle.

I pulled some lettuce from the icebox and put it in my pocket. Jubal said no turtle can turn down lettuce. Daddy says Mr. Roosevelt is a fat chest. A turtle has a fat chest. When I catch one I'm gonna pick it up and name it Roosevelt. Then I'm gonna take it to Jubal.

Jubal taught me to catch a turtle by digging a hole. The turtle has to go in the hole. The hole doesn't have to be deep. If it's deep then you can't get the turtle out.

Jubal said that Daddy was gonna yell about the government no matter what and that the only thing to do is to let him. Jubal also said that a man has a right to make a living and that you have to stand up for yourself because Mr. Tillman put the worker on the stretch out and didn't pay him what he was due. Jubal said the strike would work, but Daddy says see it didn't. Jubal said that Mr. Roosevelt would make the mill do right, but Daddy says he won't ever. The mill is everything around here.

First I dig the hole and then I put the lettuce around it and then in it. Jubal said that the turtle will eat the lettuce on the outside and then fall in the hole trying to get the rest. I'd fall in a hole too if all I ate was lettuce.

One time in church I got dizzy and I fell down and spilt the offering plate. When I woke up, I saw Mr. Tillman putting a quarter in his pocket.

Jubal said a turtle can't get out of a hole once he's in one. Daddy says that we're all in a hole now and that Mr. Roosevelt can't get us out.

When I catch the turtle I'm going to name him Roosevelt because Jubal said he was doing a good job as president even with the strike. Daddy says the government doesn't help the mill workers and that Mr. Roosevelt tells lies. He says what happened is what happens when you turn your back on Mr. Tillman and the government turns its back on you.

In church, the preacher said the strike was wrong and that unions were red like the devil, but Jubal told me that the first strike was when Moses led the children of Israel out of Egypt. Moses had a brother and he had a stick he could turn into a snake. One time at the creek we saw a snake but Jubal chased it away with a stick.

Jubal said there's men at the church who are with us and there's men who are against us. Daddy says the preacher is in Mr. Tillman's pocket.

A turtle crawls in the dust like a snake but it's not a snake. It falls in the hole I dug just like they fell in the holes Jubal dug. I lean over and pick it up and it's gone inside its shell. It feels cool like the water in the creek but not cold. When I fell over in church Jubal took me to the well. He poured the water on his hands and then rubbed my head. It was cool and safe.

I can see its head and its feet through its holes and I turn it around and look at it all over. It's green and has lines in its shell that look like the lines on the ribbon Jubal was wearing. He gave me a ribbon and I have it in my pocket.

I need to go to the church because that's where Jubal is today.

I can feel the turtle moving in its shell.

Jubal went to the strike because he was a worker, and it was the right thing to do. That's what Mama says. He went to the strike, and Mr. Tillman was there and he had his men. Daddy says that Mr. Tillman's men are yankees, that's how low he'll stoop. Daddy says Mr. Tillman is a snake crawling through the dust.

It's hard to get to the church from the creek without Jubal. It's harder more with a turtle in my hand. So I put him in my overalls. His fat chest is against my chest. There's a big hill with bushes and little trees growing out of it. Jubal used to grab on the branches and put his feet on the roots. He would pull himself up with one hand and then help me up with the other. He told me I could do it. He said I could grab onto the roots and pull myself up the hill. That way I don't have to worry about balancing and grabbing for the trees.

I have to get to the church and give Roosevelt to Jubal and get back home before Mama knows I'm gone. Right now everybody's ready to yell.

Getting up the hill is hard to do. I grab onto the roots like Jubal said. Some are big but some are small and don't stick much out of the dirt. I can feel my belly against the hill and I pull and I pull and I feel the weakness in my blood. When I'm dizzy things move like they're not supposed to, but I can feel Roosevelt cool on my chest.

Jubal said the men wearing ribbons were union men who weren't there to fight but there were other men who was. They weren't our men and they fought with the yankees Mr. Tillman brought down because he's low as a snake. And Mama says that when the fighting started it didn't matter if you was wearing a ribbon or not. Jubal said Mr. Roosevelt would help us, but Daddy says he didn't because he was a fat chest like the moose in Italy. I've never seen a moose, but I've seen a snake and it's not like a turtle at all. I caught a turtle named Roosevelt and he has a fat chest. I'm going to give him to Jubal.

Jubal said a ribbon meant you were with the workers and that was all of us. If you wore a ribbon, then you were striking, but you weren't fighting Mr. Tillman's men even though they're bad. Daddy says that there's men striking not wearing ribbons but they're not one of us. He says they're making the trouble and Mr. Roosevelt will never help us. There was the fighting and then there was the shooting and Jubal was wearing his ribbon.

When I get up the hill, I can see the church. My belly is covered in dust.

When I come up the hill some of the men from the mill are leaving the church. They're far away and they're getting in the back of a truck and they have their rifles. And there's other men and they get in a truck too and they have their rifles. And then I see Daddy coming out of the church and he has his rifle and he's walking the way he does when he yells. And he gets in the front of the truck with the other men and I know they're driving to the mill.

Before I get to the church I get to the well. Jubal took me to the well when I fell down in the church and he took the water from the bucket and put it cool on my head and my face. I put Roosevelt on the edge of the well and take the water from the bucket and rub it on his shell. He's cool like the water and smooth like the dirt at the creek that Jubal showed me how to dig.

I've seen them dig a deep hole at the church and there's no getting out.

In the churchyard I can see Jubal. The lines are in the dust where the hole was dug and put back. There's the stone and it doesn't say Jubal yet. Mama says it will soon, she promises, but there's no money to get it done. Daddy says it's because of Mr. Tillman that it's there at all. I put Roosevelt on the dirt and he crawls over the dust. A snake crawls through the dust but a turtle's not like a snake at all.

There's a ribbon in my pocket and Jubal gave it to me. He wore the ribbon on his shirt but there was men who wasn't wearing one. Jubal told me that sometimes a turtle won't fall in the hole no matter what but if he doesn't then don't you push him. Because a turtle's like a man and you've done enough by digging him a hole.

In Their Rightful Place

Joe Ponepinto

Almost from the start I feared it would turn out this way with Coraline. She had Nia's sweetness, her smiling eyes. She was a happy child, not afflicted by the melancholy she might have inherited from me, and her simple, joyful ways gave me hope I could see her grow within the gentle contours of family — watching the relatives fawn over her, listening to debates over which of them she resembled most. But from the first test results I could never shake the nagging thought that one day she'd be taken from us. Love and bloodlines don't count in the evals, and with each disappointing report I looked for differences and deficiencies — justification for me to care a little less, which might make this day easier. In fact, it's made it harder.

My little girl has a wad of cotton candy as big as her head, and the sugar strands cling to her face and dress while she experiments with different approaches to eating it.

"I'm a mess, Mommy," she says, and giggles.

Nia says, "It's okay, sweetie," and uses the excuse to draw her close and wipe the stickiness from her face. She lingers at the task, staring into our daughter's eyes as she works, and takes so long to do it that Corie begins to squirm, trying to break free of her caress. I tap Nia on the shoulder to get her to stop, but she ignores me to tell Corie that she needs to stay neat for the ceremonies ahead. "You have to look pretty for later," she says. I hear the catch in her voice as she speaks.

Corie has no idea why we're here, except to have fun — a group birthday outing, a new tradition I explained, for children about to turn five. There must be a hundred families here today from all over the county, so why shouldn't she believe it? With all the little ones wandering nearby, I thank God Nia hasn't betrayed her emotions. Despite our instructions and the months of preparations, I'm afraid she'll start to cry. But how could I expect her not to? A mother's connection to her child starts before birth. She intuits the child, feels what she feels, and the love she bears is selfless, unconditional, greater by far than the bond she feels for her husband. As much as I love Corie, in my way, I know I can't feel the depth of Nia's anguish, can't experience this day of letting go with anything like the same pain.

For the fathers, nervousness clouds the event — I see it masking the faces of the other men here. Calling this a festival doesn't help any of us feel at ease. Men of every size and strength, we paw impotently at the edge of the clearing and hold onto our spouses. This field used to be covered with grass — a ball field once, in my youth — but since we started using it for the exchanges, it's been worn to dust with only a few patches of green. No one has bothered to maintain it. No one plays here anymore. The sun bakes what's left of the grounds into concrete, even as it blinds us with its intensity.

Nia and I have worked for a year to numb ourselves, knowing that this parting might happen, that it likely would happen, and tried to shift our loyalties to the good of the state. But now I see my wife fight herself to keep it all inside. I've never told Nia that I voted for the damn thing before Corie was conceived. Back then, it seemed so reasonable, so necessary — our country was in such trouble, standards had fallen so low. And we could never have a child, or so the doctors told us.

But now I feel nauseated, realizing I made a terrible mistake that I can never rectify. They'll take our little girl, put her with a family more suitable to her limited potential. Never mind that we could pay for tutors and special schools. They'll have us spend that money on a child who can shine and grow to serve the nation. Save it from a life of poverty and ignorance — a better match all around. The government still insists, and these days their enforcement of the law is far more severe.

Some of the children run among the food and game booths, too young to understand the implications of this day, fooled by the colors and the cartoons tacked up along the wooden fences. They trample the ground and the dust they raise hangs in the dead air, which adds to our discomfort. Corie wants to join those kids, pulling at her mother's hand, and Nia holds her back for as long as she can, claiming she doesn't want to have to clean her up again later. This, I've come to believe, is one of the subtle differences between our daughter and the two of us, that she would jump into this chaos on impulse, oblivious to the strangers and her own safety, where we, even at our child's age, would have stayed back, assessed first, weighed the possibility of danger and our parents' wishes. The evals reveal these traits before the child can verbalize them. Reactions to types of music and other stimuli form a baseline. They test every six months to confirm. Results so far have tended to verify the methods, if one believes what the state publishes. And we have become a stronger nation, the experts claim, more innovative, more productive, capable once again of competing in the international arena. Crime and violence have decreased they say. Opportunity and hope for everyone, whatever their origin. Or maybe the relentless state marketing has conditioned me to believe this.

I notice other children standing with their parents, or parent — the state does not discriminate — while the others run wild. These are the quiet ones, less boisterous by nature, or perhaps they know of the exchange and share the adults' unease. Our new son or daughter is among them, I'm sure. For now we know nothing of this child. We are not allowed to — and we have no wish to know. Not yet. We need to get past our loss first. There will be a file on the new child to direct us, of course, when the time comes. It will lay out our duties and expectations, every step defined to ensure the child fulfills the destiny the government has determined. The bastards leave no room for interpretation, no margin for creativity. They spell out the repercussions if we don't comply: penalties, careers lost, banishment to the Montana camps. And then they expect us to produce geniuses who will spend their lives in thrall to government projects. Who would have thought this could happen here? I find myself wishing we could go back to the way it was before the ballot, before the neocons took over.

Nia could still keep Coraline here with us despite her pleas and fidgeting, but when a group of rough children swarms close to us, their shouts like animals, our daughter twists and tugs harder. "Let me go!" she cries. She's always been like that. But this time her words work like a knife, and Nia releases her. Corie runs into the fray without looking back. She grabs the hem of another girl's dress and spins her into the dirt, and they begin to wrestle. With no fear now that Corie will see, Nia cries. I want to comfort my wife, but my hands and voice fail me. I am left to stand and watch her, frozen with shame. I want to cry too, but the tears refuse to come.

An unseen announcer calls for assembly. His voice over the old-fashioned loudspeakers sounds hollow and evil. Soon even the most reckless of the children return to family, the great authoritarian call enforcing the will of the population. Barkers pull the shades on their booths. A roving clown ducks behind a tent, his day's responsibilities over, no one left to entertain.

"The family of Matthew Espinoza…"

The voice provides no directive, but the family knows to step forward into the clearing, to the marked place.

"The family of Janelle Meyers…"

They stop ten feet from each other. The boy is tall for his age and stands straight, almost defiant. He chafes at the buttoned collar and tie his mother has dressed him in, and looks as though he's always fought confinements. The girl has long hair that lifts and frizzes in the slight breeze, and she puts a hand up to control it. She wears a tattered sweater, despite the heat.

I shift my focus to the fathers. As with our family, the resemblance from one generation to the next is clear. I half expect to see the girl's father hold back a smile, some gladness that his child will have a better future in a new, more appropriate home. From the boy's I look for anger, outrage that his son will be consigned to a life that, at best, offers irrelevance, and at worst predicts decades of want, and a spiral downward into a cold and desperate end. But both faces seem penitent, and I understand that each of these men went through the same rationalization as I, the same anguish when his faith in the system betrayed him — the same shame when he realized how little he had valued his family. With his eyes each man promises to revere his new child, and implores the other to reciprocate.

The mothers, however, won't concede so easily. Each does her best to take some control over the situation — mothers until the last second. Each eyes her counterpart, assessing the other woman's ability to care. One wears an expensive summer dress; the other makes do with shorts and a blouse as tattered as her daughter's. But appearances and the circumstances of her child's new home don't factor into this judgment — that's out of her hands. Each mother looks into the heart of her sister, her rival, to measure the capacity for love. The women take their time in this review, as though they had the power to veto the decision. But in the end it's all for show, something to fall back on when this day is recalled, a way to claim she didn't let the child go without her approval, that she had some say in it. The government handles those details, though. Once they announced the vote — the overwhelming vote they claimed, proof of our nation's terrible inequity and their mandate to implement the exchange — they devised safeguards. None of these people will ever learn the fate of their children. The law is clear. I agree that if it must be done, this is the only way.

"Proceed. Step forward and exchange documents."

The families hesitate for a minute, mothers and fathers holding their children, each member putting anxiety aside long enough to create a last memory. A pair of burly monitors in dark glasses sway behind the first row of the crowd, ridiculously conspicuous. There are only two today instead of the usual three. Their weapons bulge beneath the cheap suits they wear. Their faces advertise the contempt towards us that they would gladly demonstrate, given the chance.

The voice cracks through the loudspeakers again.

"Proceed."

At last the fathers step forward and shake hands. They exchange envelopes and back away, neither inspecting the contents. The Espinozas embrace their son. The Meyers, their daughter. Then they gently nudge the children to cross over. As they pass, the boy and girl look into each other's eyes as if acknowledging a sibling they will never know. Each walks shyly to the other family.

"Welcome your new child, and celebrate the growing strength of our nation. With each exchange we place a child in its proper home, and improve who we are as a people."

Who speaks this nonsense? If I knew where he hid I'd find him and smash him to a pulp.

Both fathers have the good sense to go down to a knee to welcome their new family member. The mothers, too, make the effort, although each watches her true child as it's received into the other family.

"Don't they like their children?" Corie's question catches me by surprise. We should have prepared her better for today, should have done something to show we endorse the exchange, that it's part of the way we live now, and make her want to participate. But how could we burden her with the knowledge that we might someday let her go? How could we face her each day and claim to love her?

She's scared. She watches as the parents walk their new children away from the clearing. When the girl tries to turn back, the Espinozas keep her from looking, as instructed. Their lives are all about the future now. Origins must be forgotten, or they'll interfere with learning and growth, with the needs of the state.

Nia puts her hand on Corie's shoulder. She leans against me, and I see her lips quiver as she fights the tears. "Those kids are just visiting," she says. "They get to find out about other people and other ways. But they'll come back after a while."

My daughter takes my hand and holds it tight. I burn to tell her the truth, but all I can do is add to the lie. "Maybe they'll get to go home in a couple of weeks," I say. I hate my voice as soon as I hear it. It reminds me of the lackey on the public address.

"No, they're not coming back," Corie says.

It's my turn to go down to one knee. I hug her, and she tries to pull away. I whisper, "You have to understand, honey. Those kids' families weren't the best for them. Moving to a different one gives them a chance to live a better life, to be happy." Maybe for one of them.

"Is that what's going to happen to me too?"

Nia puts her arms around our daughter and starts to cry again. "There's nothing we can do, baby," she says. "If you don't go they'll take you away from us anyway. They can make Mommy and Daddy go to jail."

Corie is crying now, too. "I don't want to go away."

I'm a fool and a failure. I've convinced myself that my daughter doesn't belong with us, and pushed my wife to do the same. I remember when they proposed the exchange. What an opportunity to help the unfortunate, it seemed. A chance for true equality at last, after so many decades of empty promises. And I was the saint, the intellectual, self-righteous in my conviction that I knew what was best for all. The possibility of the irony of today never occurred to me.

Nia and Corie look to me, as though I have some power to awaken them from this nightmare. The sun beats down stronger, erasing the last bit of shade by the booths, and I feel the skin on the back of my neck begin to burn. The announcer calls the next two families.

When Corie turned four, we understood that time grew short. Nia insisted we teach her, try to influence enough of a change on the last two tests that she might stay with us. We worked almost every night as mentors, praying that the knowledge we drilled into her might have some effect on her psychological tendencies. Reading, math skills, far beyond what children were expected to know at her age. But as soon as she learned, she seemed determined to forget. Then piano lessons for a month, but she never advanced beyond the simplest fingering, until she refused to practice even one more time. Punishment. Praise. She fought us every day and cried to be allowed to play outside like the other children. We screamed at her to concentrate, demanded intelligence until she would curl into herself on the floor to escape. And after all that effort, the same result. The test said she belonged somewhere else, not with us. I'm haunted by the question of whether we tried so hard for her, or for ourselves. There's no measurement for how much we love our child.

The announcer calls the twenty-ninth pairing. There's still time. I take Corie and hoist her up in the crook of my elbow, and she wraps her arms around my neck. Slowly, I step backwards, letting the crowd fill in the spaces we leave behind. Nia sees us and follows, not too closely to avoid attention. In a minute, we stand at the back of the assembly, staring at the families as the next exchange hypnotizes them. Why don't more of them refuse? Surely some others don't wish to go through with this, and pray they can hold onto their child. There must be another father who feels the sting of his inadequacy and the need to right himself again, to find the courage to act, to deny this edict, the state be damned. But no one moves. Assembled like this, each adult concedes responsibility to the group, and waits to be told what to do. The government knows this, and each year adds more booths, more diversions into the mix, more regulation to ensure compliance. I feel a hatred for these parents, almost as great as the loathing I have for myself.

But from here, what? The monitors survey the crowd for any deviation. They are our sheepdogs, and if we detach from the main group they will pounce. Already one seems to be looking in our direction. Even without the third monitor to triangulate their efforts, I'm too afraid for my wife and daughter to try and make a run for it.

Even if we did, and somehow made it outside the festival, where would we go? Certainly not home or anywhere we're known. And no one who's traded a child away would have sympathy for us. If we ran we couldn't stop — we could take the car only so far and then have to steal another to try to hide our movements. We'd become petty criminals, fugitives with no place to wind up. We'd have to drive and find a way to get past the militias at the border, and then keep going until we'd crossed into Canada. Maybe there we could take a flight someplace remote, seek asylum, hope to find a community of others who'd escaped, if such people exist. Surely they must.

Hope is a child in the arms of her parents.

We begin to meld back into the group. But from the clearing comes a cry. "No! I won't let her go." A mother's love has reawakened. "She's our daughter and no state can take her away from us." The woman pulls the child from the exchange and starts to run with her towards the far end of the field. With only two monitors, one must address the crisis in the clearing, while the other stands at the front of the crowd to make sure no one else becomes involved. But the husband doesn't go with his family. Instead he blocks the first monitor, wrestling with him to give his wife more time. She can't move very fast with the child in tow, but she has committed to this. The second guard moves in to help his comrade. I know the parents will fail. Already the monitors have begun to overpower the man. One beats him while the other sets off after the mother and girl. He will have them within a minute, as soon as he gets close enough to fire. I hear the warning shot.

It's our chance now.

My nod to Nia is all she needs to see. We move behind a canvas game booth where the vendors have packed their supplies and left them for the next day's exchange. I keep Nia and Corie in front of me, directing them to go behind the booths while I make sure the view from the clearing remains obscured. We walk quickly, but carefully, trying not to make too much noise or stir up dust that might give us away. The festival fence looms behind the last row of booths, eight feet high at this point, more like a wall. I'll have to go up halfway and help Nia to the top, and when she's on the other side I'll pull Corie up and send her over. The entrance to the gathering was on the opposite side of the grounds — we can't go back towards the parking lot, and I have no idea what lies on the other side of this barrier. I see trees, but does that mean the shelter of woods, or just a buffer to a neighborhood where the residents might notice strangers on foot and call us in? Either way we'll have to negotiate our way to transportation. We haven't moved, yet we're already lost — I am lost — I've led my family into a dead end. I led them there years ago. But I can't tell them we must go back to the clearing and submit to the exchange, not yet.

I turn towards the fence, looking for the best place to get a foothold. But before we can move I hear a noise from the end of the row. Nia hears it too and we freeze. The monitors couldn't have seen where we went. But it's the clown, stepping out from behind the last booth, his flaming wig gone to reveal a bald head, his face paint only partly toweled off. He's still wearing his costume and giant shoes, and has a cigarette clamped in his teeth, a look that makes him more ridiculous than when he entertained the children. He shuffles closer and takes a long drag, and then flicks the butt into the dirt. His superiors would probably reprimand him if they saw him like this.

"Help you folks?" he says.

I don't like him. He has the hungry lean of a criminal. "We're looking for the facilities. For the girl." It's all I can think to say although the outhouses are in plain sight by the clearing.

"Not sure how you could miss them."

His face bears the sunburn of many days like this, performing for the kids, getting them into a mood that will make the proceedings go easier. I can only imagine that his job causes him no guilt, that he's fine with each day's outcome. I doubt he cares whether the children find him amusing or not.

"She wants a real toilet," Nia says. "I wouldn't mind finding one myself."

"Can't help you there. Festival grounds got no plumbing."

"Yeah," I say. "That's what I told them. But, you know how it is…"

The clown pulls a phone from his billowing pants. He brings it to his face but doesn't touch the buttons.

"Girl's a cute one. She got your eyes, ma'am."

Corie hides behind my leg.

"I got a boy," he says. "Turned five a month ago. He's real smart for his age."

Corie pokes her head around my leg and asks, "What's his name?"

"You don't want to know that, little miss. Today's not a good day for remembering."

"You had to let him go," Nia says.

"I'm supposed to be over at a kids' party now, but I just needed some time. I was thinking about when we used to play when I came home from a gig. The new boy we got is a lot like me — rough and all. Never listens." He brings his free hand to the phone. "But he's just not mine, you know?"

Nia pleads, "Can't you pretend you didn't see us?"

"Where you gonna go? You can't go home, not if you run. I thought about it. Maybe everybody does when the time comes."

"We'll go someplace," I say. "We don't care where. Just to get away from here."

He looks at the fence and shakes his head, as if to doubt we could make it over. "Can't help wondering how my boy's doing with them other folks. Probably has it good. Eatin' good, great school…" He laughs, softly. "Bet he sleeps in a bed bigger than me and my wife's." He puts the phone back in his pants and pulls his pack of smokes, drawing one out with his teeth. "Makes me proud to know he made it, you know?"

Two dull pops echo in from the clearing. A woman screams. We all freeze for a second.

I pick Corie up again and hold her close to me. Even she understands now there's no getting away. I expect her to cry, but instead she looks at the clown, at his sunburned head. "He's okay, mister," she says to him. "Your boy is okay."

The woman who ran has been caught by now, wounded or perhaps worse, her daughter transferred to the other family. If they survive, she and her husband will go into custody; the child they would have received assigned to a holding center until a suitable substitute family is designated.

That shouldn't take very long.

Nia takes Corie's hand in hers and I carry my girl back towards the clearing. No one noticed our absence, and we settle into the back of the crowd.

"The family of Coraline Ryan."

So soon. I'd hoped we'd have a few more minutes. When we move forward the other families make a path so we can pass. At the exchange point I set Corie down in front of me. Nia kisses the top of her head. We are both calmer than I expected.

"The family of Tariq al-Hassan."

From the center of the remaining families comes a boy wearing a blazer too large for his body, perhaps a hand-me-down. His parents follow a few steps behind, their gaze not yet meeting Nia's and mine. The mother wears a black dress, as though attending a funeral. Then I remember that in Middle Eastern cultures the color for a funeral is white.

I put my hand on Corie's head and stroke her hair. Nia begins shaking, and soon it is so hard I'm afraid she'll collapse and bring the monitors on us. I put my free hand around her and she buries her head in my shoulder, and I let her stay there while she sobs. Corie doesn't turn around. My hand has slipped to her back, and I feel her fear as well.

"Proceed."

I will fight this law, somehow. How could we have chosen to live like this? There must be some people working to reverse the vote. I will find them. And if we're unsuccessful, then maybe it's time for violent action...

"The exchange of the documents. Proceed."

The father already has his envelope in his hand. When they get to their place they stop and compose themselves, standing stiffly, unsure of just how they should act. Who can say their love for their son is any less than ours for our daughter?

Finally, Nia stops crying. She dabs at her eyes, pushes up against me, and then takes my hand. We take a step back from Corie.

Tariq's mother touches the boy on his shoulder, and nothing more, offering no other goodbye. The boy straightens, and raises his eyes to mine. I go down to one knee.

A New Song

Dr. Anne Lauppe-Dunbar

Sarah stumbles from Julie's bedsit, bathed in a soporific smoke. Coughs a dry mouthed 'bye' to Leanne whose umbrella is busily turning itself inside out: wind is one thing, but a gale? Leaves skitter across the neatly mown grass in Singleton Park. Nervy of the coming winter, trees sigh and stretch their branches toward the warmth of Brynmill's central heating. Empty swings moan, a seesaw bashes up down as Seagulls waltz through whirling sleet. Nestled by 'The Pub by the Pond', a paddling of ducks are camouflaged to look like puce lake water. Eyes closed, beaks raised to the wet heaven, they await salvation as dripping geese nibble and honk at the luminous grass, turning as one to squawk and snap at Sarah's legs as she cycles, eyes glued. Gobby bird crap and tyres don't mix. Through the fogged windows families hunker in one of three cwtches, elbows at right angles, chins pinking at the £4.99 roast with a side order of onion rings and a pint of the best — tuck in. Her crowd inhabit the darkest crook and throw down beer laced with vodka chasers.

"Alright luv?" Emma rolls up her sweatshirt, waves a ropy arm, the latest tattoo: *'roses r red violits blue and I luvs u'*. "Sweet or what? Proper poet Jared, he is." Her angular nose drips as her bony arse edges from the seat. In the moulding toilet Sarah rolls her last tenner, wedges the clean end up her nose.

"Fiver a line." Emma traces a line of brown powder laced with white chalk: see-through, insubstantial.

"Don't be such a stingy cow."

"It's good, mind."

"Not that good." Like dandruff, the tell-tale signs of chalk powder are dotted, left, right. Emma chops out a minuscule more as Sarah, nose to mirror, inhales. Oh, the trickle of liquorice and burnt toffee. The burn against soft flesh. Drip drip into her throat. Takes the edge off at treat.

"Tidy as. No bother, and I mean, No Bother." Martin and Dave puff up their latest trip. Cardiff's ripe with deals to be had lacing speed with coke, smack with henna. Dave itches his balls as Sarah strokes his weedy thigh. Round the back of the pub, he hands her a sticky black globule of opium, size of a pea. "Prime," he says. Her or the opium? She rolls down her leggings, leans against the wall. He's soft; a wet whisper between her legs. Hands milking her breasts. His semen reeks of dead fish. Bum wedged in a sink of warm soapy water she cleans up, slips inside the orange warmth of the pub for the last round. In the honeyed bask of opium she drags out her tatty bike, refuses a lift, taxi, or the offer of Dave's bed for the night (he'll only want to do it again and he's never thought to change the sheets) and climbs on. Home. The main road is roaring with evening traffic. Red light. The aubergine bendy-bus whines round the corner. Rear wheels catch the oily puddle. Water jettisons, soaking her legs in a vertical sheet. A small child with elephant ears presses her nose to the window. Grins. Blows a circle of steam as she lifts her middle finger. Sara lifts two. Across the bay the fires of Port Talbot herald the setting sun. Townhill windows blink back their nightly Norse code, a magician's trickery. The red light cranks (could they get any slower?) to green. Across the road, bumping up to the cycle track; the wind bosses the grass: left/right. Bike wheels crawl. A storm roars up the track, sand dancing, leaves skittering. A lone magpie negotiates a gorse hedge, swerves and plummets to vibrant green. A seagull tap-dances, feet drumming a signal to a burrowing worm. Curlew's ruffle and tweet. Wet through, legs straining, she watches the waves churn and moan. A lone Scottie drags at a wooden log the size of an oak. Stops. Growls, digs in rear legs: pulls. The owner is a blue scribble on the beach. Scottie yelps, squirts yellow pee over nasty log. Scampers. The horizon stretches: endless, changing. In Blackpill Café she orders a toasted teacake. Rita and Jane are huddled in their usual place by the window. They turn: pale blue, brown eyes in complete accord. Rita, lover of all that is Dylan, likes to open conversation with her favourite quote of the day. "'[1] ... china dog and rosy tin teacaddy...'" she says. "I'll be Mam." Janet pecks at her lined floral notebook — letters sorted into regimented lines. Sarah bites into the oozy give of butter, not catching the drip of fat. Her poetry? Well. Words whirl, twist. Screech to a halt.

    RooKs

        swim

            through the air,

                a five feathered spread.

Would that be haiku or a poetic phrase? Best not to ask, Rita's face has tightened to a dried raisin.

"Latte and a biscuit," Janet purses thin purpled lips, "Biscotti."

Rita beaks into her cup, long nose, bony shoulders craning toward imminent fame: "Earl Grey?" she says to no one in particular. Her coat is downy as seal skin, freckled with fake hair. It holds the contours of her, elegant, well read, body.

"Hot Chocolate. Oh." Sarah points out the margarine stain on her jumper. Her fleece is ruined. Handy in this strange threesome: her and the perfect two.

"Haiku? Seven/five/seven." Rita. Never deviate. Stay on course.

"Yes, but it could be in the style of..." Janet's chancing her luck.

"Really? Are you sure. Are you certain?" Rita bares her teeth. Argument one must be put to bed before argument two. Sarah coughs.

---

1   *Under Milk Wood,* Dylan Thomas

Tepid hot chocolate sprays. Neither pay attention.

Outside the snow is all brown melting. The warmth of Dave's opium fudge is clearing to reveal a crystal sky.

"And your haiku, or whatever? Did it? Did it?" Janet and Rita. Beady eyed, expectant: pick pick.

"Sorry, must pee." In the smartly decorated loo, the small window beckons. She almost lands on the peroxide blond waitress who's having a quick fag. "Paid have you?" Sarah nods, furiously, backs away. Where the hell is the bike? "Can't blame you, mind." The waitress exhales a ball of white into the fresh spring air, flicks ash with long orange nails. "Those two. Like a pair of razor blades, they are."

The beach unfolds like a picnic blanket. Families parade their young. A miniature child hurtles on her pink scooter. A baby mews and fusses under layers of soft blue wrapping. Magpies chortle: one for sorrow, two for joy. Oh, how the trees are aching towards the weak spring. Seagulls dive for Dave Davies salt and vinegar chips. A crab scuttles under a stone. Sarah narrows her eyes, squints across the bay at the flames of Port Talbot, Mumbles pier: a toffee apple on the end of a stick, Bracelet. Crowds of daffodils nod to the wind. Boys scrape wheelies up/down on the bike ramp. Traffic light reefers, get smashed, swop stories of late night shags, fags and how dull dull dull life is; blind to the promise that murmurs beneath their feet. Sarah pushes on, legs pumping. Mumbles winks and beckons. Nearly home. Ripples Café is heaving. Ginny and Rob sit out in the sunshine, lapping at raspberry ripple ice creams. Sarah waves as they stand, leaning like geriatric cranes over the small wall. She pulls over, smiling at their kind, shaking, grey seal-like heads. "There you are, cariad," they say, "burning the candle at both ends?"

Inside the café a table is arranged as encouraging yet confrontational. Wait. The ice cream counter has gone and Rob has melted from a kindly nodding raspberry ripple, to a man with a professorial gaze. Sarah has had a tendency to knit language. Words swim through her mind, burgeon; explode into hot tarmac motorways and dead ends. Archaic pain. Fresh-faced joy. A peewee tucked under Dai's arm.

"What might you mean," he asks, "by 'archaic pain?'"

Ginny eyes entreat 'No oblique denial. No vacuous explanation. Go for detail.'

Sarah remembers that other life, pin-eyed on smack. The slap of the everyday is a harsh pill.

Sarah and Ginny link hands under the table like schoolgirls as Rob holds the world in his right paw. She's read that in France such procedures are public, the audience free to attend. Thank God the customers of the Ripple are immune to the pretences of a Doctoral viva. They peep and chatter. Munch croissant and Welsh scones, Barabrith, mussels and crab.

"You never?"

"Eye candy he is, mind."

"I wouldn't mind."

"Carol!"

"You've seen my Vern. A fish out of water around a woman's body, he is."

"Archaic pain..." Sarah breathes, mind circling as whirl-pooled seaweed. Five years of scampering question marks, completed in one moment of execution. Rob leans back, his glasses catching the golden evening light as she waits for those words to stop being hard as pebbles in her mouth. Her answer arrives on the back of a dry cough. The second is wet with promise and she's putting one foot in front of the other, moving forward, not backward, running full tilt towards the end and the beginning.

Outside the summer evening is so torrid the birds can barely fly. The pavement radiates. Her heart pounds out a new story: it is done, it is done.

Up the hill and across the road. The door latch catches, then gives. There is a distant echo of laughter — from the garden? The door to the back, weary with decay, is firm, newly varnished. Tulips, lupines. Is that a begonia? stand in neat rows. The windows sparkle. Dump the bike against the wall. Tiptoe. Peep. Robbers have stolen her house, taken the aging hunk of it and twisted it to new.

Two girls in bluebell dresses whirl. Deckchairs are positioned like chess pieces. A table is laden with glasses and jugs of floating mint. Call the police? Demand an explanation? Maybe she's come to the wrong house? Ginny! What is she doing here, and why is she crying, then loping over the (well-cut?) lawn?

"Well done," Ginny hugs her, then mops tears as Rob pats her back in a parochial manner. A man stands by the trestle table. His quiet eyes considering her disarray; mucky stained jeans, flip flogs. The lunchtime shag a wetness in her knickers. But wait. Her jeans are clean. Her shirt a soft lemon. Hand on stomach she feels ribbed stretch marks, a memory of pain. The girls have stopped whirling. They shriek; red/gold hair streaming as they race across the grass. She catches her husband's eye, smiles, then wraps an arm around each of her daughter's pinking sun-kissed skin.

NON-FICTION

Three Belmont Sketches

Robert Boucheron

Mrs. Zucker

On a Friday morning in June, the telephone rings. I work at home, people call at all hours, and I try to be ready for anything.

"I want to move a wall in my house three feet," Mrs. Zucker says. "Can you tell me if that's feasible?"

We arrange a visit at the end of the day. I pack my black bag with a steel tape measure, a large pad of paper, two pencils, an architect's scale, and a digital camera. I am like a doctor who makes house calls, but I go to examine the house, not the patient.

The day is hot when I arrive at an enclave developed in the 1960s. It is now run-down and overgrown, about thirty small houses. Some have become rentals. Buckingham is close to major roads, yet off the beaten track. The loop road is narrow with no shoulder. I park with two wheels on the grass.

Mrs. Zucker's house is a cottage set back from the road and downhill. A shaky metal ramp extends from a garden gate to the second floor at street level. The front yard has two Southern magnolias, with the ramp running between them. As instructed, I enter the screened front porch. It is crammed with old furniture, household gear, cardboard boxes and car tires with a narrow path to the door. I tread cautiously and knock.

Mrs. Zucker is seventy or older, fair, and close to six feet tall. She wears a bold flower-print top and short red pants. Her thin gray hair is a mess. She uses a metal frame walker.

The house inside is as cluttered as the porch. Old carpet is wrinkled like a mountain range in a relief map. This trip hazard does not faze Mrs. Zucker.

Mrs. Zucker and her husband moved here when the house was new. At some point, the stairs were removed, and the house was converted to two apartments. She lives on this floor, and a tenant lives below with his own entrance. Framed posters allude to the late Mr. Zucker's interest in foreign films.

"This is the wall I want to move," she says. It is the interior wall between living and dining. She wants to make the living room, to which the front door opens, a bedroom. If the wall moves, the front door will open to a living-dining room, which in turn opens to a kitchen in back. The kitchen is filled with piles of junk, dirty dishes, and a large potted palm. I smell spoiled food and a clogged drain.

"I need to check the structure," I say. "Can I see the floor below?"

"The tenant is supposed to have twenty-four hours notice, and he's particular about that sort of thing."

"Is there access to the attic?"

"You'll need a ladder. The pull-down stair is jammed."

The attic hatch is in a tiny hall. I fetch a wooden ladder from the porch, carry it through the house without hitting anything, and wedge it into the hall. I brush aside electrical cords that drape the ceiling like vines in a jungle. I force the hatch open. The plywood is swollen from the hot, humid weather. I shine a flashlight in the stifling gloom.

Batts of pink insulation and piles of junk hide the joists, which are what I want to see. I see the rafters and no evidence of leaks or damage. I descend and wiggle the hatch back into place. In the living room, I reach up high and tap on the ceiling. On my hands and knees, I pull up a floor grille and peer down. I open closets. I get out my tape measure and take dimensions. At last, I announce my findings.

"The joists run front to back, which means that the wall is not load-bearing, which means that it can move. For a builder to work, you'll have to clear the space."

"I was away for a few weeks, and my son John came and dumped all his belongings here, because he had to leave where he was living. He was diabetic. He went on a bird-watching hike, and the exercise got to him, or the heat. He said he felt dizzy and he wanted to lie down. He died of a heart attack."

Mrs. Zucker points to a bed nearly buried in the living room. She bends over her walker, which has a framed photograph lying face up on the little seat. Is the photograph of her husband or her son?

"I ought to go through things," she says, "discard some and donate some to charity, but the task is more than I can face right now."

All the seating is full, so I perch on the upholstered arm of a chair.

"I'm sorry for your loss."

Mrs. Zucker picks up the framed photograph, holds it to her chest, and sits on the seat of her walker. In her bright costume, she is rather lively.

"I also want to enclose the porch, make it into a sun room. To compensate for losing the living room. The house has no curb appeal."

"Do you want to sell it?" I wonder if she wants to move to a retirement home.

"No." She produces a page torn from a magazine, a real estate photograph. "Can I add stone to the outside? Is the structure strong enough?"

"This picture shows veneer stone, an inch thick. The walls of your house are concrete block. They can easily support it."

I collect my things into my black bag.

"If you want to pursue a project," I say, "hire a builder who specializes in remodeling. It can be done without drawings, maybe without a permit."

"Can you find your way out through the debris?"

"Yes, don't get up."

I carry the ladder to the porch, where I found it. Bag in hand, I exit via the ramp like a passenger disembarking from a ship, from a cruise to nowhere.

House Finch

In the middle of July, as the temperature rises above ninety degrees Fahrenheit, the central air conditioning in my cottage struggles. Like the house, the system is old. It can't keep up.

Tuesday evening at seven thirty, after chugging all day, the fan shuts off, the outdoor motor quits, and the electronic thermostat inside goes blank. I resist an urge to panic. The nighttime temperature drops into the sixties. A reprieve — but something must be done.

Wednesday morning, I phone three contractors for heating, ventilating and air conditioning. One has serviced the cottage for years. Let us call this one A. I have worked with contractors B and C on construction projects. The owners know me and may take pity. This day and the next, each company sends a man to check it out.

The airmen from B and C believe that the outdoor box should be replaced. It combines a gas-burning furnace and a refrigerant condenser coil. It is called a "package unit." The ducts in the crawl space probably leak. But the package unit can be oversized to compensate for inefficiency. Replacing the ducts is optional. Air leaks at windows and doors, as well as poor insulation in the walls and attic, also decrease efficiency.

Wednesday night is cool. My luck holds. Then my plotter fails, the large printer I use for architectural drawings. It needs a new print head, which takes a week to order and install. Then the computer I use for drafting sputters to a stop. I take it to a high-tech clinic for diagnosis and treatment. I did not plan a summer vacation, but I am getting time off anyway. Or is my life cascading to a halt?

Airman A is the last to appear. He says the whole system should be replaced, including ducts. His company is busy, and the earliest he can schedule new work is two weeks out. But he has a stash of window unit air conditioners to tide customers over, like loaners for car repair. If I sign a contract, he will deliver two loaners, for front and back.

Thursday night, the temperature drops to eighty. Friday is broiling. The weekend weather forecast is more of the same. By five o'clock on Friday, B and C report with a price. At six, after the close of business, A emails he will get back to me on Monday.

Saturday and Sunday are brutal. No trees shade the house, so it bakes in the sun. I open all the windows at dusk, but the air is still. Not so much as a puff. The house becomes stifling. I check the thermometer outside, as it rises to one hundred. I drink lots of water. I hover near a little electric fan. I sweat. At night, unable to sleep, I wander through the house and onto the front porch.

On a column capital, a pair of birds built a nest and laid three eggs. By day, the birds flee every time I step through the door, and they chirp at me from a nearby fence rail. The size of a sparrow, the female is a light mottled brown, and the male has a fiery red head and upper body. According to *Familiar Birds of North America,* published in 1986 by the Audubon Society, this bird is the house finch, *Carpodacus mexicanus.*

> The population established today throughout much of the eastern United States is descended from caged birds set free on Long Island in the 1940s ... Song is a clear, canary-like warble, ending in an ascending *zeeee.*

Before the heat wave began, the eggs hatched. By day, I see the parents feeding the babies. By night, as I stagger outside to breathe, there is no sudden flight. Maybe darkness is a refuge. I imagine the baby birds huddled in their nest, warm as toast and silent.

It is too hot to cook. I make sandwiches, nibble on snacks. The refrigerator works overtime in the oven-like house, but it works.

Monday is still hot. By noon, A emails a proposal and price. He can deliver the loaners at lunchtime. Desperate for relief, I am on the verge of accepting, when C phones. He can get delivery of a package unit the next day and install it on Wednesday. C's price is considerably lower than those from A and B. I decide to tough it out for two more days. A is playing a nasty game, while C is doing me a favor.

Wednesday morning dawns fresh and dewy. A pickup truck arrives as I eat a bowl of cold cereal. In the bed of the truck lies a shiny metal box, my new package unit. A team unloads it. Three stay behind to remove the old unit and install the new one. They include Brian, a large bearded man, and a blonde woman who might be a biker gal. By lunchtime, they are almost done.

After lunch, they reappear with some necessary part that was missing, caulk the main duct housing at the stucco wall, and then they really are done. Brian crawls in the crawl space. He emerges draped with cobweb and says there is nothing wrong with the ducts. They are properly strapped to the joists and sealed. We agree to wait until fall to test the gas furnace. As the afternoon sun beats down, Brian starts the air conditioning. The package unit hums.

Morning and evening, I listen for the house finch. "Sociable birds ... they are also cheerful singers." But I hear nothing. When I stand on a chair to look, the nest is empty.

Turkey Vulture

Five or six big ugly birds perch in the dead tree at the corner of Montrose Avenue and Rialto Street. A few more perch on the roof of the house below. They line up on the ridge like some ghastly ornament. A few more lurk in a tree behind, leafless now. There are over a dozen of the somber, bald, ungainly birds. They are turkey vultures, *Cathartes aura,* also called buzzards.

Their feathers are black or dark gray. The head is small, with bare red skin, and the bill is short and hooked. The legs and feet are bare, with orange skin stained white from defecation. On my morning walks, I often see the turkey vultures gathered like this in a silent conclave. They recall a troubled night, a mist that dawn has not yet dispersed, a bad dream that lingers in the mind.

A group of vultures is called a kettle, venue, volt, wake, or committee. On the whole, I like the last, as it calls to mind the citizen boards before which I defend architectural projects. This is their first appearance so close to home, the first time they have chosen the dead tree. They have an affinity for bare, bleak places, for skeletal branches that offer a good view. They may be warming themselves in the sun, or they may be pondering their next move. Apparently, they live here in Belmont, or in woods to the south by Moores Creek.

Vultures are neighbors we try to ignore, like the straggle of trailers along the creek. We dislike the way the birds hang their heads and hunch their shoulders, the way they idle like juvenile delinquents. More sinister than surly teens, they make no noise. They lack a syrinx, the vocal organ of birds. At most, they groan or hiss when disturbed.

We object to what they eat — road kill, dead animals, and nasty garbage. Yet as scavengers, they perform a service. Their name in Greek means "cleanser" or "purifier," from the root that gives *catharsis,* the term for how a tragedy affects our emotions. Though unheroic, vultures play a role in the drama of nature, the ongoing production we call the ecosystem. They remove dead bodies that spread disease and offensive odors. We ought to thank them, but who ever does?

The turkey vulture is clumsy on the ground. Heavy, it makes an effort to take off. Airborne, with a wingspan of five to six feet, it sheds the ugly image. It is skillful and graceful. From *Familiar Birds of North America,* published in 1986 by the Audubon Society:

> This large carrion-feeder is commonly seen sailing over open country-side or gliding on shifting currents of air as it searches for food. In flight, the turkey vulture holds its wings in a slight V above the body, with its outer wingtips spread wide like the fingers of a hand. Silvery gray wing linings are conspicuous in flight, making the wings appear two-toned.

For years, I watched them soar above the tree-clad city, and I thought they were hawks. It seemed they could stay aloft for hours, riding thermals of warm rising air. They flew so high, in wide arcs with each other like an aerial ballet, I wondered how they could they see their prey. All the while, I had it dead wrong.

The turkey vulture will eat flesh-like plant matter like pumpkin and coconut, insects like cicadas, and fish that wash ashore. It prefers, however, the recently deceased. It picks up the scent of ethyl mercaptan, a gas produced by the onset of decay. It shuns a carcass that has reached the point of putrefaction.

Birds that rely on the sense of smell are unusual. The black vulture, *Coragyps atratus,* which is slightly smaller, has better eyesight and a weaker sense of smell. It hangs out with the turkey vulture, which has a stronger bill. They find their meals and feed together in a kind of cooperative. The black vulture will also eat eggs from a nest and kill small animals. A woman walking her dog on a leash informs me of this. The dog is a toy breed with short hair, nervous, as well it may be.

We humans, with our penchant for symbols, see the vulture as a bird of ill omen, a harbinger of death. We read into nature our fear and disgust. Some species are endangered in Africa, where farmers kill them with poison and guns. They have few natural predators, though they fight with jackals over a carcass. In North America, the turkey vulture is neither threatened nor a threat. But the woman with the dog hates them on sight.

"What if the vultures settle on your rooftop? How will you make them shoo? If I had a gun, I would shoot them."

Six Cents a Tray

Janice Westerling

Three months after Bobby Kennedy's assassination, change was in the air, along with the musk of marijuana smoke, at my Central Valley college. Like many students in the crowd, I'd washed and rewashed my bell bottoms from the army-navy store; still, the stiff denim chafed my thighs. Onstage, at the outdoor amphitheater, a red banner with a black Aztec eagle, the symbol of Cesar Chavez's farm workers' movement, rippled in the warm September breeze.

Unlike the other middle-class campus protesters, I'd held the wooden handle of a grape-cutting knife in my hand, its curved blade sharpened to silver. I'd tasted the yellow dusting of sulfur pesticide and seen the squalid field toilets and wages paid in cents instead of dollars. Since leaving home, I'd learned the world wasn't as simple as my parents had portrayed. I wanted to work for justice and end farmworkers' oppression, but in my family Cesar Chavez was no hero. My dad was a grape grower.

A Chicano youth in a khaki shirt paced back and forth on the stage, pumping his hand-lettered sign: *Boycott Grapes!* His dark eyes and bronzed skin stirred a memory buried so deep I hadn't thought of it in thirteen years.

The summer I turned six, Mr. Sanchez rattled into our farmyard in his banged-up truck, his August arrival as predictable as the blistering sun. No first name, just Mr. Sanchez. Dressed for the fields, he had jazzed up his blue jeans with a silver belt buckle and cowboy boots. Dad strolled out to meet him but didn't invite him into the kitchen for a cup of coffee as he did his friends. With the sunlight glaring off the windshield, they conducted their business standing beside the visitor's truck.

"When can you pick at my place?" my father asked. Mr. Sanchez and his Mexican crew harvested our Thompson Seedless grapes every year.

Standing in the shade on the porch stoop, I studied the two men a few feet away. Dad's voice sounded casual, but the cords of his neck were as taut as guitar strings.

"First week in September, maybe as late as the sixth," Mr. Sanchez said. Dad nodded and the two of them shook hands. A deal had been struck.

My father had warned me not to bother the Mexicans, but the first morning of harvest, I lingered alongside a row where the C-shaped back of a laborer was visible under the vines. At sunrise the canopy of leaves was cool as a cave, but soon his shirt would be stuck to his back. He lifted his heavy pan and emptied the grapes onto a paper tray on the ground to dry. Dad sold his raisins to Sun-Maid.

From the corner of my eye, I caught a shape, a movement, in the shadows near the barn. I walked closer to investigate and saw a boy filling burlap-wrapped canteens with water from our outdoor faucet. I was puny for a first grader, but he was a couple of inches shorter than me, with a narrow chest and brown legs jutting from his cutoffs like knobby twigs. When he grinned, his blocky front teeth gleamed against his dark skin.

"Wanna play hide-and-seek?" I asked, clapping my hands over my eyes and pantomiming, "One, two, three…" Then I opened my eyes and waited. He shrugged, held the sloshing canteens to his chest, and dashed into the vineyard to deliver the water to his farmworker parents.

"*No puedo,*" he told me when he reappeared, shaking his head and pointing at the house. I frowned, puzzled. When he waved his hand toward our equipment yard, I understood he wanted to stay close to the fields and not go near our house. My new friend didn't speak much English, but we had little problem communicating. His name was Nachi.

"You hide first," I said, waving him off as I covered my eyes for ten counts. "Ready or not…" Opening my eyes, I blinked, blinded by the bright sun. Nachi had disappeared. I tried following his tracks, but the trail went cold in the confusion of footprints around our tractor and forklift. I looked in the shed, atop the stacks of wooden lugs, and then re-circled the barn. After five minutes of futile searching, I began to think he'd slipped back into the vineyard.

I was ready to give up, when I heard a muffled cough. I followed the sound to the weathered outhouse that served as the pickers' toilet.

I tiptoed toward the privy and whispered, "Nachi?"

No answer.

I rapped my knuckles on the wooden door. Silence.

After checking behind me, I eased the door open, gagging from the ripe stench and fat, lazy flies circling the cutout seat. Nachi sprang from the tiny room's dark interior and fell onto the dirt, coughing and laughing. Dumbstruck, I stumbled backward. He jumped up and hoisted his arms in the air, dancing and grinning, until I giggled too, conceding his stinky victory.

Nachi's energy was contagious. My summer had been long and solitary, and I imagined days of Hardy Boys adventures alongside my new playmate.

"What next?" I asked.

He tagged me on my arm and ran toward the vineyard, willow-limbed and quick. I raced behind him. As I gained ground, Nachi veered into a row of unpicked grapes.

"STOP!" I yelled.

Before the harvest, my father had terraced the vineyard. A weighted sled, which he pulled behind his tractor, compacted the soil to support the paper trays and drying grapes. Even our dog Tippy had been tethered to a tree so he couldn't romp in the smooth rows. Nachi's bare feet left deep prints in the dirt.

Nachi twisted his head and laughed.

"No, Nachi! I mean it! You have to stop," I screamed as he snaked down the row. When he saw I wasn't chasing him, he slowed to a trot, turned around, and began trudging back.

"NACHI!" I jumped at the baritone shout behind me.

Nachi's father, short and wiry, was wearing a long-sleeved red flannel shirt, too hot for the weather, and a straw hat. He spoke to his son in strident Spanish. Nachi dashed toward a beige station wagon, as piebald with rust as a paint horse.

I turned back to the vineyard, my stomach churning. Nachi's footprints pocketed the groomed row. Dad would be furious. Hoping to avoid him, I dawdled among the farmworkers' cars as they unpacked their food for an early lunch.

They had arrived at dawn. Although our backyard, shaded by mulberry trees, was twenty degrees cooler than the vineyards, no farmworkers came near our house. Peeling back foil from burritos, the men crouched in the steamy shadows of their trucks or huddled beneath the vines where they had worked all morning. In the backseat of an open car, a mother from the field nursed her baby. Toddlers played nearby in the sand, tended by an older sibling. Parked in the sun all morning, the hothouse vehicles had baked the food like ovens, and I smelled fried corn oil, beans, and onions inside tortillas. My stomach growled.

Moments later, my mother called me into the house for lunch. I was halfway through my tuna sandwich when Dad came into the kitchen, his brows pulled into a scowl.

"Janice, were you running in the vineyard today?"

Dad must have seen Nachi's footprints in the dirt, too big to be my younger brother's. I swallowed a couple of times, trying to dislodge the bread wedged in my throat.

"What's the *matter* with you?" he chided. "Rain will pool in your footprints under the trays and spoil my raisins. You know better than that."

I did know. Feeding a family of four on his hankie-size farm of twenty acres, Dad had no margin for error. Mildewed grapes could mean the difference between a new pair of school shoes and resoling my scuffed oxfords.

"Janette," Dad said to my mother, "give Janice some chores and keep her inside this afternoon." I started to protest, but then shut my mouth. Explaining my innocence would mean tattling on Nachi.

I dragged a rag around the coffee table and bookshelves in the living room. Mother turned on our rotary fan to stir up the hot, stale air, and dust motes swirled in the sunlight. I knelt under the dining table to polish its legs, but quickly tired of my chores. I wondered what Nachi would think when I didn't show up that afternoon. Tomorrow I'd make it up to him, I vowed to myself. Maybe I'd give him my prized cat's-eye marble.

Dad's angry voice broke my reverie. I crept to the open window and peeked outside.

"Your picker is manhandling my grapes!" My father was fuming at Mr. Sanchez. He shoved a cluster of fruit at his crew boss. "The skin on these berries is broken. That bunch is spoilt. Set him straight."

Mr. Sanchez scolded his worker in guttural Spanish. The picker shivered like a whipped junkyard dog. With a start, I realized he was Nachi's father. For a moment I hated Dad for shaming him. My face burned.

My house arrest ended late that afternoon, and I rushed outside. The pickers had finished for the day at three o'clock, packed their children and ice chests into their vehicles, and driven away. Dad was walking past the vines, holding a clipboard. I approached him, kicking up dust.

"Howdy, Jan," he said. "Wanna help me count the trays?" Relieved to be back in his good graces, I skipped to match his long strides.

At the end of each row, the farmworker had penciled his tray count onto the corner of the paper, along with his initials. Pay was piecework, six cents a tray.

"These families make more money picking grapes for a month than the whole rest of the year combined," my father said. "Back in Mexico, they live like kings."

With my child's radar, I sensed Dad was stretching the truth. As far as I knew, he'd never been farther south than Los Angeles. To me, the Mexicans looked more like hobos than kings, the men and women dressed alike in dirty jeans and faded shirts. Under wide-brimmed hats, the men wore handkerchief drapes which protected their necks from sunburn and hid their faces.

I decided not to risk the patched-up rapport with my dad and held my tongue.

The next day, I woke early and dressed quickly, anxious to reconnect with Nachi. When I rushed to the kitchen window, I saw an empty yard. There wasn't a car in sight. My heart thundered like a kettledrum. Breakfast forgotten, I ran out the screen door. Dashing past the barn, I spotted a handful of cars parked on the apron of the road half a mile away. Then I remembered that the workers had finished picking near our house and had moved on to the western field.

The cracked asphalt of the road was firm under my bare feet in the chilly dawn; the afternoon sun would melt it to viscous tar. I recognized Nachi's rusted station wagon and headed toward it. Bracketing my hands around my eyes, I pressed my forehead against the window and peered inside. Nobody, only a jumble of stained pillows, ragged blankets, T-shirts and jeans, and a rubber-tipped baby bottle. On the dashboard, a plastic Virgin Mary bowed her head over the unholy mess.

I scanned each row where mothers and fathers knelt under the vines, looking for Nachi. Children old enough to wield a knife worked alongside their parents.

Halfway down a row, I spotted a slim boy with a curved-blade knife dangling on a leather cord from his wrist. Legs wide apart, he bent over a paper tray, spreading out grape clusters. Twenty yards away I couldn't make out his features, but I called to him anyway.

"Nachi?"

The boy jerked upright and then glanced at the soles of his father's work boots poking from beneath the vines. Nachi looked at me, shook his head back and forth, and waved me away in a jerky overhand motion. His legs jumped as if he were dancing on hot coals. As his father pushed his grape-filled pan from the foliage, Nachi turned toward me and slashed his hand across his neck in a cartoon gesture of slitting his throat. Then he ducked under the vines.

Stung by my playmate's rejection, I turned away and walked along the dusty shoulder of the road toward home. But I stopped short when I passed the row where Nachi's footprints roped through Dad's perfectly groomed soil.

I suddenly understood Nachi's gruesome pantomime. Yesterday his father had been chewed out by Mr. Sanchez for manhandling the grapes. The farmworker couldn't risk being linked to the boy-sized footsteps in the dirt. He could lose his job, so he kept Nachi camouflaged among the pickers. Because of his dad's fear, I'd lost my playmate.

I kicked a dirt clod to smithereens. It all felt so unfair.

All morning I lingered by the barn, hoping Nachi would return to fill his canteens and I could tell him he was safe from blame. But he didn't come. The next morning, I resumed the vigil for my playmate, but he never showed up. Already the sun had bruised the drying grapes, and the smell of fermenting wine hung in the air.

Dad's entire harvest for the year was on the ground. Rivers of green grapes filled hundreds of parallel vine rows, our family's cash flow. The Mexican farmworkers moved on to another grower's vineyard.

For a few weeks I thought about Nachi every time I pitched my cat's-eye marble. I wondered what had happened to him. The next year, I looked for him during harvest, but he hadn't come back. Then I forgot about him.

"*Huelga!* Strike!" The chants of Chicano students near the stage jolted me back to my college campus.

The young man on the dais, his shirt darkened with half-moons of sweat, walked to the microphone and shouted, thrusting his sign into the air: *Boycott Grapes!* Five hundred students and a handful of long-haired, hip professors took up the chant. Some of the boys had discarded their shirts, and pendants with pewter peace signs hung against their naked chests. Alongside a stand of aspens, a barefoot girl in a tiered gypsy skirt danced on the grass to music inside her head.

The Chicano youth at the microphone looked about nineteen or twenty, the same age Nachi would have been. I knew now that Nachi's father had had everything to lose. Dad could replace a careless Mexican with another desperate for work. As a farmworker, he'd had no face and no voice.

Giddy with rebellion, I shouted, "Boycott grapes!"

Suddenly, a fracas broke out below the stage. A man in a brown beret set a match to a cardboard Safeway box filled with green table grapes picked by nonunion workers. Flames blazed. White ashes twisted into the air and floated over the crowd.

The sons and daughters of farmworkers in the crowd cheered as smoke billowed from the torched Safeway box. The fire meant an end to their jittery dances of fear, like the one Nachi's father had passed down to his son.

To me, the smoke smelled like harvest's end, when my father gathered his paper trays into haystack-size piles and burned them to the ground. Each year, with his raisins boxed and stored in the barn, safe from rain, he no longer dialed up the weather report during breakfast and every night before bed. The slashes of worry between his eyebrows disappeared, along with his searing headaches. When the heat broke, he took our family to Three Rivers for a picnic lunch and bought us fresh-picked apples from a roadside stand. In October, he donned his Sunday suit on a Saturday night and pledged 10 percent of his income to the First Baptist Church with thanksgiving instead of blind faith. After his check from Sun-Maid arrived in our mailbox, he drove me downtown to the Bank of America, and I handed his deposit to the lady teller, whose high heels rat-a-tatted on the marble floors. For one more year, my father had enough money to feed our family.

"*Huelga!* Strike!" The chanting of the crowd grew louder and louder, but the words died in my throat. My mother had gone back to work to make ends meet. Dad was a small-time farmer, yet here I was with my wild hair and denim bell bottoms, ready to sell him out.

As the Chicano boy on the platform throttled the mic like a rock star, I walked to the edge of the crowd. I wanted to work for justice and end oppression, but that wouldn't be as simple as changing clothes. I slipped away from the protest, alone. "Boycott grapes!" the loudspeaker echoed behind my back, but a different revolution raged inside me. I'd pushed my old dresses to the back of my closet and tossed my Central Valley rural legacy into deep storage, to be examined later. I had one foot in the farmworkers' movement and the other at home in Dad's vineyard. That year, as the gulf between my two worlds deepened, I felt like I would split apart.

Mastrovito's Game: A Lifer's Parable

William C. Crawford

Infantry soldiers in the Nam detested lifer bullshit. Except when we were in direct contact with Victor Charlie, our top priorities focused mostly on beer, drugs, mail, and sex — depending on personal proclivities.

Written regs and proper military procedures were dismissed as absurd aberrations valued only in strack garrison life back in The World. By 1969, growing anti-war sentiment and the hippie drug culture had infiltrated the ethos of our jungle-based infantry.

Changes in our lifer leadership — company commanders, platoon leaders, and senior NCO's — were viewed with true trepidation. We were primarily draftees, and we followed orders (for the most part) in combat, but many grunts nurtured grave doubts about the competence of the Green Machine.

We knew from chilling experience that we were just obscure cogs in a fucked up military apparatus that clunked along in pursuit of aberrational combat and foreign policy objectives. Our superiors daily passed down sketchy orders reinforcing the widely held axiom that inside the Machine shit flowed downhill even as we resided at the bottom.

As our First Sergeant (Top!) rotated to a new assignment, we imagined a big impending shit storm. A new Top fresh from uptight stateside duty could pose real trouble. Things might even permanently tighten up! We prepared for his arrival with apprehension. Some grunts hid their grass in stashes around Landing Zone West. A few shaved for the first time in weeks. Peace signs, hippie jewelry, and anti-war slogans on helmets disappeared.

Top arrived precisely on schedule: sawed off and very Italian. Fast talking, raspy, and really loud! He would meet us en masse at an early morning formation. Our collective anxiety approached grief!

We stood at disheveled attention in our assigned platoons. No officers in sight, just us enlisted stiffs. An early arriving Chinook strafed us with stinging grit and dust from its powerful prop wash.

As the big bird finally lifted away, we were still locked at attention waiting for Top's next (first!) move. He puffed up to his full 5' 6'' and thrust out his barrel chest with ceremonious pomposity. (Here it comes!)

From his inflated, keg like body we heard these words grating from deep within his chest: "Mastrovito is my name," he roared. "And masturbation is my game."

Hardened combat vets laughed until we were bawling. Somewhere down the adjacent bunker line a cassette player boomed out Joe Cocker. It was, after all, 1969. And we were still alive, unsafe most of the time, and trapped in the Nam. But we were laughing with a squared away lifer.

For the Tree – For the Road – For Life

A. Raymond

Whenever I start to think about it, I can't help smiling. If I keep thinking, recalling details, sorting through heartbeats, it becomes difficult not to laugh. At that instant, it was as slow and as fast as everything needed to be to survive. East of Austin, Nevada, a billboard says: *What Happens in Austin, You Brag About.* Austin is about three streets between muddy folds of rock and eight Trump window signs.

The roads were dry today. In the valleys, the banks had turned soggy, but on the winding switchbacks up and down the mountains, altitude and shade left dirty white barriers on the downslope sides. Silence is a coyote track in the snow.

Past Austin, before you get to the monster at Middlegate, there's a tree at the muddy Eastgate wash, a forty foot, sprawling thing that doesn't fit in the vast landscape. A thousand steps hang from its branches, and a thousand have fallen in the bushes and sodden dirt below. Rather than throw them, or failing to hook their laces, some mounted their soles on fence spikes. Half of them probably came the same way we did, though maybe not exactly the same. Have you ever done something because you read it in a story? It's the only reason we were there.

Before that billboard, miles before, we met a face of the grim reaper. We are three humans and two dogs in a '94 Silverado. This truck took scars from a guardrail down the left flank a couple years ago, and this time it was hauling nearly everything I own, including my soul in a fifteen pound wondermutt. Hauling plus five thousand pounds, taking a blind curve to an eight percent grade and I don't know if I ever knew what disbelief was until that heartbeat.

Middle of the morning, valley sun-soaked below, the mountain's last buck thrown shadow over us on the road and maybe a hundred yards, no more, to that face. Bright orange, eighteen-wheeler — is he really oncoming, in our lane? I felt eye to eye with that grill and fifty yards disappeared. No ABS in this Chevy, no brakes on this trailer — tires lock and new rubber goes bald. I'm not the driver, and that's a detail that matters. The steering wheel twists 180° four, five times in twenty feet as my brother fights to keep control on the edge of no control. The snow bounces the trailer back onto the road once, then twice.

The road grader keeps coming; if he'd stopped, or if he'd slowed ... there's that disbelief — then there's the aching impossibility, that massive trailer trying, five people willing that trailer to follow the orange cab behind the grader into *that* lane. All gravity downhill, slow, so slowly merging, and there's only four feet between the back of the trailer and the edge of the road until the moment the nose of my brother's truck needles through. Nothing hits; nothing breaks.

My brother rages. The girl beside him is silent. I light a Black & Mild, wine smoke, wood tip, pass it forward. The dogs keep napping.

ABOUT THE CONTRIBUTORS

Poetry

Jeffrey Alfier

Jeffrey Alfier won the 2014 Kithara Book Prize for his poetry collection, *Idyll for a Vanishing River*. He is also author of *The Wolf Yearling, The Storm Petrel* and *The Red Stag at Carrbridge* (2016). He is founder and co-editor of Blue Horse Press and *San Pedro River Review*.

Douglas Cole

Douglas Cole has published three poetry collections: *Interstate* (Night Ballet Press), *Western Dream,* (Finishing Line Press), and *The Dice Throwers* (Liquid Light Press), as well as a novella, *Ghost* (Blue Cubicle Press). He received the Leslie Hunt Memorial Prize in Poetry, the Best of Poetry Award from *Clapboard House,* and First Prize in "Picture Worth 500 Words" from *Tattoo Highway*. He is currently on the faculty at Seattle Central College. His website is douglastcole.com.

Seth Copeland

Seth Copeland's work has most recently appeared or is forthcoming in *Grey Sparrow Journal, Oklahoma Review, Crab Fat,* and *Cuento*. As an undergraduate, he was the two-time winner of the John G. Morris Poetry Prize awarded at Cameron University. He lives with his wife in Oklahoma City.

Sarah Davis

Sarah Davis has lived in Oklahoma City for most of her life. She has been passionately writing poetry for over six years. Sarah finds most of her inspiration for her poems from her memories of being raised as the youngest child of a single, widowed mother alongside four other siblings.

Lenny DellaRocca

Lenny DellaRocca's chapbook, *The Sleep Walker* is available at Night Ballet Press. His new chapbook, *Blood and Gypsies* is forthcoming from Anaphora Literary Press. His poems have appeared over the decades in *Poet Lore, The Laurel Review, Nimrod, Seattle Review, Fairy Tale Review, Albatross,* and *The Potomac: A Journal of Politics and Poetry*. He has work forthcoming in *Blueshift*

Journal, Blue Fifth Review, Waterways, The Bitchin' Kitsch and *Black Heart Magazine.*

Justin Hamm

Justin Hamm is the founding editor of *The Museum of Americana* and the author of a full-length collection of poems, *Lessons in Ruin,* as well as two poetry chapbooks. His work has been selected for *New Poetry from the Midwest* and the Stanley Hanks Memorial Poetry Prize from the St. Louis Poetry Center.

Alex Hughes

Alex Andrew Hughes lives and works in Los Angeles. He splits his time, depending on his mood and the weather, between his training in clinical psychology, his research in existential crises, and his fiction, poetry, and sketching. Sometimes, however, he does absolutely nothing, and he enjoys that time the most. His poetry has recently appeared in *Thin Air, Clackamas Literary Review,* and *Firewords Quarterly.*

Davis Johnson

Davis Johnson is a poet, songwriter, and author of children's literature. A former motivational speaker, he teaches writing, journalism and speech at Springfield Technical Community College in Springfield, Massachusetts. In his spare time, he can be found on the links playing disc golf, and is the former world record holder for Frisbee distance. Three poems of his appear in a recently published anthology, *Silver Lining — Poets Against Violence.*

Rebekah Keaton

Rebekah Keaton earned her Ph.D. in literature from Michigan State University and is associate professor of English at Niagara County Community College, just outside of Niagara Falls, where she teaches creative writing, American Literature and composition courses. Her poetry has appeared in numerous literary journals, including *Poemmemoirstory, Common Ground Review, MoPoesias, Blueline,* and *Earth's Daughters.* She has been nominated for the Pushcart Prize. She lives in Buffalo, New York with her husband and twin sons.

Sara Schraufnagel

Sara Schraufnagel is a writer from Minneapolis currently living in Chicago. Her poems have been published in several online and print publications, including *The Legendary, Uppagus* and *Aleola Journal of Poetry and Art*. Her writing can be found at sincerelysaras.tumblr.com.

Stefan Strychar

Stefan Strychar was born and raised in Detroit. He left Michigan after college, and in 2011 earned an MFA in creative writing from Fairleigh Dickinson University. He spent the next year as a poetry reader for *The Literary Review*. In his travels since, he has completed an MLS in archives management, interned at Harvard and MIT, released three albums of music, and studied black and white film photography. He is currently the Poetry Editor for the *Forest for the Trees Journal*.

Visual Art

Morgan Bradley

Art has always been a passion of Morgan Bradley's and always will be. She loves seeing the excitement in people's eyes when they've been inspired by her work to go on and create art of their own. She was very young when she started creating pieces, but age doesn't matter. It's never too late to find your passion in life; you just have to embrace it.

Nina Nga Nguyen

Nina Nga Nguyen was born in Saigon, Vietnam. During high school, she got perfect scores on her AP Studio Art Portfolio twice as a junior and senior. She has received numerous awards and commissions, including First Place Senior Art Portfolio - Young Talent in Oklahoma, State Superintendent Awards for Arts Excellence and Krylon Clear Choice Art Competition. She is currently a sophomore majoring in Studio Art at the University of Central Oklahoma. To develop her skills, she plans to get a master's degree in studio art, own a studio, and sell her work.

Lexi Piper

Lexi Piper is a graduate from the Studio Art program at UCO where she emphasized in Photography. She is currently living and working in Oklahoma City as an artist. www.lexipiper.com

Sarah Volner

Sarah Volner is a twenty-seven-year-old photographer and full-time mom from a small town in Western Oklahoma. She has been doing photography for about six years now, and has recently opened a studio in her home town. When she's not working, she enjoys trying new food, relaxing with a glass of wine or traveling and making memories with friends and family.

Fiction

Riley Bounds

Riley Bounds was born in Oklahoma City, Oklahoma. He currently resides in Edmond, Oklahoma, where he currently attends the University of Central Oklahoma, majoring in English with a focus on creative writing. He cites books of scripture and the writings of Cormac McCarthy, Flannery O'Connor, and A. E. Housman as primary influences.

Dr. Anne Lauppe-Dunbar

Dr. Anne Lauppe-Dunbar is a full time lecturer in Creative Writing at Swansea University, Wales. Her first novel *Dark Mermaids*, tells the story of the doping scandal in the Former German Democratic Republic through a young woman's search for home. The novel was shortlisted for the Impress Prize in 2012, and is released with Seren September 2015. She has short stories in the named Seren anthology — *Sing Sorrow Sorrow, First Edition Magazine, The View from Here, Islet Magazine, The Swansea Review,* of which she is co-editor, and *Bristol Flash Fiction.* Her poetry is published with Cinnamon Press, Leaf Books and Seventh Quarry. A number of conference papers are published with Atiner, Gender Forum, the NAWE and eSharp.

Joe Ponepinto

Joe Ponepinto is the author of the novel *Curtain Calls,* and the short story collection *The Face Maker.* His fiction has been published in dozens of literary journals in the U.S. and abroad. Joe lives in Washington State with his wife, Dona, and coffee-drinking dog, Henry. He is the fiction editor of *Tahoma Literary Review.*

W. Scott Thomason

W. Scott Thomason is a native of Winston-Salem, NC, and holds an MFA in Fiction from McNeese State University. He is also a graduate of UNC-Greensboro. His stories have appeared in *Broad River Review, Flying South, The Lindenwood Review, The Louisiana Review, The Roanoke Review,* and *The Sierra Nevada Review.* He lives outside of Philadelphia with his wife and two dogs.

April Vázquez

A native of the North Carolina foothills, April Vázquez holds a B.A. in Literature and Language from the University of North Carolina at Asheville and a M.A. in Teaching English as a Second Language from the University of North Carolina at Charlotte. She currently lives in León, Guanajuato, Mexico, where she homeschools her daughters, reads, and writes. April's work has been published or is forthcoming in *Windhover, Connotation Press, Eclectica, Foliate Oak,* and *Ghost Town.*

Non-fiction

Robert Boucheron

Robert Boucheron is an architect in Charlottesville, Virginia. His stories, essays, and reviews appear in *Bangalore Review, Digital Americana, Fiction International, New Haven Review, Poydras Review, Short Fiction,* and other magazines.

William C. Crawford

William C. Crawford was a grunt and later a combat photojournalist in Vietnam. He is currently a social worker, writer, and photographer living in Winston Salem, North Carolina. Over the past few years, he has finally begun to write about the Vietnam War.

A. Raymond

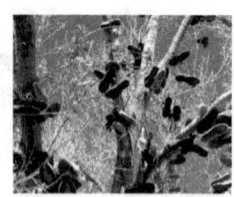

A. Raymond is a dog-lover, a UCO degree-holder, a writer and a dreamer. When we are made of star stuff it doesn't stop us from being stars. You might have to go further than the highway to see where the sky changes. She lives with possibilities and her wondermutt.

Janice Westerling

Janice Westerling is a San Francisco Bay Area writer who grew up in the Central Valley of California and studied with the late poet Philip Levine at Fresno State College. Her essays draw on the pocket-size farms and drugstore soda fountains of her childhood. Ms. Westerling's work has been published in the *Christian Science Monitor, Santa Clara Review, Reed Magazine, The Coachella Review,* and *Forge,* and excerpted in the book *Writing from the Senses* (Shambhala, 2014).